ONE TEENAGER IN TEN

This is a paperback original, first published by Alyson Publications,
PO Box 2783, Boston, Mass. 02208. Distributed in Great Britain by
Gay Men's Press, PO Box 247, London, N15 6RW.

First edition, first printing, March 1983.

ISBN 0 932870 26 0

ONE TEENAGER IN TEN

Writings by gay and lesbian youth

edited by Ann Heron

Alyson Publications, Inc. • Boston

Introduction

In March of 1980, Alyson Publications published *Young, Gay and Proud*. In the back of the first edition, we included an announcement outlining our plans to publish a book written by and for lesbian and gay youth and asking for submissions. Responses came in slowly. Editing and revision were delayed by the need to insure that letters discussing the essays could be sent without threatening each author's privacy. In some cases, the address of a friend or lover had to be used, and, in a few instances, no further contact with the author was possible.

Now, three years later, *One Teenager in Ten* is ready for publication. The title refers to the estimated gay population based on studies by the Kinsey Institute. Twenty-six young men and women from all over the United States and two from Canada talk about their coming out experiences. The authors, eleven women and seventeen men, range in age from fifteen to twenty-four. At the beginning of each essay we have printed the age, sex, and city/state of each contributor. Where only a first name is given, the author for obvious reasons does not feel free to give a last name; in some cases, even these first names are pseudonymous. The symbol ♀ indicates female and ♂ a male.

Grammatical corrections were applied sparingly; editing consisted primarily of asking for details to round out individual submissions. This is not intended to be a representative sample of gay and lesbian teenagers, but we hope that it gives some sense of what it is to be young and gay in our society today.

1 Joanne, ♀, 18, York, Pennsylvania

Recollecting my years as a high school lesbian, the images that stick in my mind are those of feeling alone, sneaking around, feeling hunted, and fighting with my parents. I felt that neither my parents nor my friends would understand my sexual choice, so I kept my secret well. I think if it had not been for the other lesbians I knew, my life would have been unbearable. By the same token, if it had not been for them, my home life would have run much smoother.

I came out to myself as a fourteen-year-old high school sophomore. My field hockey teammates had been spreading rumors that our coach was a lesbian. I felt angered that they should let such a thing influence their opinion of her. Having never knowingly met any gays, I knew nothing about homosexuality. Yet from my uneducated standpoint, I decided that the accusations were unjust.

The constant talk about gays made me curious and I went to the library to read up on the subject so I could better understand my coach if indeed she was gay. One day, a short time after starting to read about lesbians, I was sitting in English class and like a bolt of lightning, I realized that I was gay. The "bolt of lightning" line may sound rather dramatic. What happened was that suddenly all the feelings of attraction I had been having for women, and the isolated feelings about myself due to my lack of "femininity" came together and pointed to the label, *Lesbian*. As a result, I walked around like a shell shock victim for days. I do not remember the exact thoughts that ran through my head at the time, but along with fear about being a social outcast came a slight pleasure. I had always prided myself on being different and this was one more way to hold the pattern.

Soon after I decided to accept the new identity, I knew I had to find people to talk to. My first instinct was to approach my hockey coach. I imagined telling her of my feelings and her immediately confessing that she was also a lesbian. We would then fall into each other's arms and comfort each other, sharing the loneliness faced by deviants in a hostile world. Needless to say, this scene did not occur. Quite the opposite. She told me I was just nervous around boys and should make an attempt to be around them more. I was crushed. That was definitely not what I wanted to hear. Nonetheless, I decided to do as she said because at that point I thought I was the only lesbian on earth. Soon after deciding to "go straight," I got a boyfriend and went out with him three times. But I soon realized the futility of denying my attraction to women and abruptly stopped seeing him. I felt that no matter how much I felt for a man, I would always be drawn most to women.

It was in October that I realized my lesbianism, and not until the next April did I finally find someone gay to talk with. Looking back over my journal written during that time period, I recall the anguish I suffered. In it I wrote several things along these lines:

Please. Help me. Oh shit, I have to talk with someone. Help me please. My feelings are turning into gnawing monsters trying to clamber out. Oh please.... I want to just jump out that window and try to kill myself. Maybe I'll get sympathy then. Maybe they'll try to understand.... I have to tell someone, ask someone. WHO??!! Dammit all, would someone please help me? Someone, anyone. Help me. I'm going to kill myself if they don't.

Finally in April, I heard about a women's softball team that was reputed to have lesbians on it. I joined as soon as I could in hopes that the rumors were true. While playing, I dropped as many hints as I could to let the team know I was gay. I thought I was being subtle, but looking back on the situation, I must have been pretty obvious. My lack of discretion paid off though, because finally one team member felt comfortable enough to come out to me. We talked for a long time that night. In the course of talking we became friends and I grew to rely on her for a great deal of support. This woman virtually became my mentor throughout that whole summer. Everything would have been perfect except for my parents.

I had finally found people to talk with because my first gay friend introduced me to other lesbians. All were at least eighteen and most were over 21. At first, my parents merely thought it odd that I would be hanging around older people so much, or rather that they would hang around me. Then my home life fell apart when someone told my mother that my softball coach was gay.

She automatically assumed that the rest of the team was also gay and forbade me to socialize with team members. She would not let me go on tournaments overnight either for fear of what would happen in a dark room full of lesbians.

Eventually, at the beginning of my junior year, I had my first lover. She was a nineteen-year-old woman and my parents suspected the truth about our relationship so they forbade me to socialize with anyone out of high school. Since I knew no lesbians in school, the restriction was extremely unpleasant. Following the limitations, which obviously included my lover, I had to do a lot of sneaking around in order to see her. That was when most of the lying started. I would say I was going out with my friends from school and would instead meet her somewhere. At night, after my parents had gone to bed, she would throw stones at my second floor window and I would slip down the back stairs of our house to meet her. Every creak on the floor sounded like a gunshot and as I snuck out, the dog would bark because I did not let her out with me. I still cannot believe my parents never heard all the commotion. After playing Romeo and Juliet for about two months, my lover understandably got tired of sneaking about like a hunted fox and broke off the relationship. It was painful to end, but it was also a relief not to be lying to my parents so much.

Following the break of my romance, I decided I had had enough of family fights and resolved to be a perfect daughter. As an athlete I refused to smoke or drink anyway, but at that point my resolve gained a second significance. I determined that when my parents found out I was gay, they would not be able to kick me out of the house because I would be a model daughter in every other way. I stopped picking on my younger siblings, I started to work hard in school and generally did whatever my parents told me to do. They started to trust me again and I found myself once again in their favor. I made a point to develop friendships with people my own age and talked about boys as much as possible. I even started wearing skirts and dresses more frequently. One benefit of this frenzied perfectionism was an improved grade point average which allowed me to go to the college I wanted to.

I wish to emphasize that although my having older gay friends served to complicate my life, I would have been a mental wreck without them. The women I knew let me know in no uncertain terms that I was not abnormal; that my sexuality was healthy and normal. Despite this general encouragement, though, they also often urged me to lead a heterosexual life at least until I got out of high school. Few of them had been gay as early as I was, but they could easily foresee the difficulties I would face. Another reason they discouraged my lesbianism was that I was under eighteen. That meant no one would have a relationship with me for fear of being discovered and arrested for seducing a minor.

On that, they were right. Except for my one lover in eleventh grade, no one else in my area did approach me as more than a friend until I graduated from high school. Unheeding of their advice, I chose to continue calling myself a lesbian and refused to play heterosexual games. There were difficult problems involved, but it helped me to establish one identity and stick with it. Nonetheless, the mixed advice was often confusing. Fortunately, my friends were supportive for the most part. This confusion led me to write the following poem which was one of several I composed during my more trying times:

I have a problem, I feel so sad.
I'm going crazy, it's getting bad.
The friends I have that aren't like me
tell me I am wrong.
The ones I know who really are
tell me I'm too young.
How am I wrong when it's in my heart?
Am I too young when I fit the part?
I am gay, that I know,
but to my friends that is not so.
How to cope with folk like these?
Are they or I the ones I please?

The words of my friends encouraged me partially, but their lives gave me more strength. I saw their relationships with other women and for the most part, those bonds of intimacy let me see that there could be happiness in my life. I knew that these women were not the fat, ugly, man-hating butches that were so often stereotyped. I found that I could be just like everyone else in my society and still have intimate relationships with women.

I succeeded in my efforts to be as perfect a daughter as I could be, but I also managed to be brainwashed in the process. I did not realize what a pile of mush my brain had become until this year in my second semester of college. My parents found out I am a lesbian and sent me to a psychologist to be "cured". I am presently being cured, not of sexual choice, but of the way I accepted my parents' every word as gospel. In my attempt to be perfect, arguing with them was not part of the curriculum. The easiest solution to disagreements was essentially to agree with them. My parents are conservative, upper-middle-class Roman Catholics and their morals and demands reflect that background. With those kinds of values surrounding me, it was easier to accept their standards than to defend my lifestyle against them.

It has been five months since I admitted my homosexuality to my parents. Even though they both say they still love me, they harbor hope that I will one day let go of my feelings for women. I have assured them that I do not hate men and would not pass up a heterosexual relationship on the basis of my lover's sex, yet they continue to be disappointed in my decision.

The worst part is that my parents blame my older friends for influencing me. They feel that seeing older lesbians who were like "normal" people made me think it was acceptable for myself as well. Yes, these friends did help me accept myself, but they did not intentionally influence me to be gay. I was a lesbian for six months before I met anyone to talk to. My friends did not change me, they merely helped me stay sane. I do not know if I am or ever was capable of killing myself, but I sometimes think I might have done so had I been forced into three years of lesbian solitude.

My parents also feel that I was too young to make such a decision in high school. Now I am eighteen and they still think I am too young to decide that I am emotionally, mentally, and physically attracted to women. I am not, nor was I ever, too young to make the decisions I have made. I only hope that other young people like myself can have a support group to suit their emotional needs. I searched all over for any type of group to write to and when I finally found one, I was too afraid to write for fear that the organization would not use discretion when returning my mail.

I also hope that an alternative to the bars is developed to meet people's social needs. As a fifteen-year-old trying to sneak into bars where the drinking age is 21, I was not very successful. Yet when I did get into a bar, I hated it because it was superficial. On the other hand it was so nice to be there because I knew no one there objected to me solely because I was gay, and I could relax with my identity.

What high school lesbians and gays need most is the support of older homosexuals, gay people their own age, and of course, their parents. I would have been ecstatic to find a support group that recognized the existence of teenage gays... and mostly just to discover that there were others out there like myself.

2 Brandon Carson, ♂, 17, New Mexico

I like who I am. I have come to accept myself on psychological as well as physical terms. I not only like myself, I like everyone around me. Today, for some gays and especially our youth, that is really hard to say. To learn to accept yourself as you are, and then to start liking yourself completely, is an obstacle some people never overcome. That alone is tough, but to finally do that and then start living a complete and fulfilling life is really too much, isn't it? Is it really too much to ask, for us to be able to go out into society and hold jobs and pursue careers and live the "American Dream"? Should we stay closeted and have to hide our feelings, forever living in a make-believe world, hoping that no one finds out about us? The pressure is inevitably on at full force, and even the smallest decisions could radically change our lives.

When I realized I was homosexual, the first thing I did was sit down and cry. I wept for myself, but mostly I cried because I didn't conform. I couldn't be this way, because it "just wasn't right." I wondered why the same sex attracted me and why I felt desires that I knew I shouldn't. After I came to terms with my sexuality, I decided to sequester my feelings, if not for my sake, at least for the sake of my loved ones. I decided to try dating and I explored the drawers where my father hoarded his *Playboys*. If my "naturalness" wasn't going to come by itself, then I was ready to force it upon myself. I delved into anything manly. I registered for Little League baseball, Boy's Club basketball, and all kinds of sports. I started reading books about cars and engines. I stopped hanging around with my older sister. I really did some drastic things — all of which I hoped would make me do a complete turn-around and become a heterosexual.

I was fair in sports; no Reggie Jackson or "Magic" Johnson, but I played my positions adequately enough. I talked just as foul as all the other guys in the locker room and I even hung up centerfold pictures in my locker. But that secret urge to watch all the boys during showers always crept back to haunt me. I always made sure I was the last to shower, and I showered alone, for fear of the worst — an erection. After gym class I would always hang out with the guys and take part in their open lust for the opposite sex, but all the while I was tearing my mind up wondering about myself.

At this time I was fifteen and had never gone out with a girl, and some of my friends were beginning to notice this. One of my closest buddies decided to "help" me out and set me up with a nice looking girl. I hesitantly agreed upon the date and actually found myself somewhat elated at the prospect of possibly "getting laid." Well, I went on the date and time seemed to move by hurriedly. First to a movie, out to eat... then what? The girl knew I was somewhat introverted, so she made the first moves and asked me if I would like to go to the park. I agreed and we drove out there. We sat under a large oak tree and she put her arms around my body and moved very close to me. Gosh, this was foreign to me. A girl making the first move — what was I supposed to do? She started talking about something trivial, I can't remember what, and out of the blue she placed her lips upon mine and started kissing me. She opened her mouth and tried to get me to open mine. After she was unsuccessful at arousing me, she asked me what was wrong. I made up some stupid excuse and said I had to go home. She took this personally and got quite angry. After the date was finally over, I went home and laid down on my bed and cried myself to sleep.

When I turned sixteen, I decided to stop the foolish facade and accept myself completely. It was hard. I live in a small city with narrow-minded people, and there was no one to open up to. I think I really matured mentally during this stage and, of course, I had all of "this" bottled up inside me, and really yearned to tell someone. I thought about telling my family, but they would never understand; none of my friends were capable of understanding either. Who could I turn to? My last hope was God. I poured it all out to Him, asking Him if I was weird or perverted, or worst of all, if homosexuality was a sin. Although I never received a direct answer from Him, I came close to Him and felt very good after I "talked" to Him.

I started my junior year in high school with renewed confidence in myself. I came very close to God and we shared a mutual love. About this time I met a really nice young man about my age. We had most of our classes together and we became close friends during the last few months of school. I never thought of mentioning that I was gay to him, at least not then. He expressed his opinion of gays when I would casually mention the subject. He was very negative; some of his harsh words included "cocksuckers, faggots, and queers." He talked of them with utter disgust. This really hurt my insides and I was having to live the kind of life I detested — one of make-believe.

We soon became very close and he decided that he wanted to get a Post Office box so he could get mail that he didn't want sent to his home. I agreed on this and we got a box together. About this time I had met a wonderful man on the staff of the Gay Community News, and he had been corresponding with me. My mail from him was being censored at home, so I thought no harm could be done by receiving some letters from him at the box. My friend was a curious little fellow and I received a package one day that was torn at the edges. He didn't really think any harm could be done by opening the package, so he did. The package contained some books on gay youth that I had ordered. Now the cat was out of the bag.

He asked me about it and I decided to stop denying it. I came out to my best friend. I told him I was homosexual, and that I was receiving literature about it. At this stage in my life it is still too painful to discuss the consequences of his rejection. I haven't gotten over the loss of my friend yet, and I probably never will. But I've learned some real valuable lessons about life, and I've learned them early, hopefully to prevent any further losses. I've learned people are unique in their own peculiar ways and I've learned that most people are more readily able to accept old ways than they are able to accept new ones.

I could go on and discuss the loss of my friend, the painful nights crying and wondering, the disgusted looks he gave me at school, and the fact that I had to face pain too early. But why should I tell what each person has to learn by himself. That is really the sad part about all of it; we are expected to hold so much weight on our shoulders and then try to live life like everyone else. Everyone experiences pain, the emptiness of losing someone you love very much. But why should we be tormented and ridiculed? There are so many unanswered questions. Maybe someday, someone will realize what a ridiculous predicament society puts homosexuals in. Until then, I guess we must keep the faith and never stop fighting. I firmly believe that *everyone* will experience total happiness — it may only be for one minute or one day, but everyone will know what it's like to be happy, free, and independent. Shalom.

3 Christopher Hawks, ♂, 17, New Jersey

I am seventeen years old, a senior in high school, and openly gay. Homosexuality has always been a major force in the shaping of my life and personality. Learning to be myself, and to like myself, has been a continuous growing experience; one that is still going on.

It is impossible to say just when I first realized I was gay. Looking back, I can see that I have always liked other boys, but it wasn't until I was thirteen that I learned the name for my passion was "homosexuality."

Even at that point, I was not ashamed of what I was. I knew I had to be discreet, even though I didn't look like the stereotyped gay. I was never ashamed, but I was embarrassed. Being gay was not popular; it was used as a put-down quite often. So I pretended a little, and withdrew a lot, never knowing if I could ever be myself.

I did have one very short-lived romance in school, but we were doomed from the start. He was too uptight about being gay and I wasn't. But my first real affair was with a much older man, and he was a beautiful person. I grew so much from our relationship.

He shared his experience with me, and his love, and I grew. He helped me to like myself as I never did. I felt so good about myself and being myself that I decided no one was going to force me to be someone else, and thus I began to come out.

My first step was to tell a close friend of mine. After I had told her and found that she still liked me and that my gayness didn't bother her, I decided to tell some more close friends. All the people that I cared about I eventually told, or found out before I told them. My final step was to pierce my ear; that way anyone who wasn't sure that what they had heard was true could see it for themselves.

I also told my parents. It was a major step for me. My parents had split up, and most of the time I lived in Florida with my mother, but I spent the summers with my father just outside of Philadelphia. As it became more and more apparent that my mother was not going to celebrate my gayness, I became more and more tired of the charade. My one refuge seemed to be the summers, so I turned them into a permanent thing and moved in with my father.

Very little of what I expected happened. My father and I did not get along, but at least our problems did not revolve around my being gay. The best thing that came from my move was that I was now close to a big city. The city is wonderful! There are so many gays everywhere. It used to make me feel so good to go into the city and see them all living openly and happily, and it gave me strength to be myself.

Being gay hasn't always been easy. As with anything, I've had my share of hassles, but I've learned I must be myself. The times of intimacy and love that can be shared only when you are honest are far better than the many times when you pretend to be what you are not.

One example occurred very recently. It was graduation night and everyone was going to a party somewhere. My friend had one and I showed up a little early and we had some champagne. But that was only the beginning for her. As the night progressed, she got totalled and went to another party. But she left her house with over one hundred people there still partying. So her boyfriend and I took over. I became D.J. and he started to bounce some unwanteds. Pretty soon the party was really jamming. I was dancing and I had gotten most everyone up on their feet too, and the party was a smash. Afterwards, some people came up to me and said they were sorry they had let a stereotype get in the way of getting to know me, and that I was really OK.

Well, after that, I wondered just how many friendships I had lost by not being myself, for surely honesty will make me more popular than any person I could have manufactured and presented.

This was just one of the times I could have never shared had I not begun the life-long process of coming out; a process that has provided me with a sense of self-worth and self-confidence.

4 Gary Dowd, ♂, 20, Irvine, California

Life is full of little ironies. My particular favorite at this moment concerns my parents. My parents keep telling me that life will be horrible as a gay person, since I will be constantly badgered by society. The irony is that they do more badgering than anyone else. Though to be honest, the situation is not as bad as it may seem; in fact it's pretty good. Overall my coming out was well received. This was due partially to planning, and partially (I'm embarrassed to admit) to luck.

Despite my occasional sloppiness, I was never "discovered" before I came out, so I was lucky since I could come out when I wanted to. A friend of mine did not have this luxury and it made life pretty tough for him. His parents started screening his phone calls, wouldn't let him go out, and made him go to a psychiatrist among other things. As time went on, things improved, but it serves as a reminder of how dangerous the situation can be if coming out is not done carefully.

Before I came out, the idea kept running through my head that once you come out, you're out for good. Yes, people might pretend that you never came out, even *you* might pretend that you never did, but if everyone pretended that the sky wasn't blue, it wouldn't change the color. Keeping this in mind, I knew that when I came out I had to do it well, so I started my research.

I didn't exactly go around with a clipboard taking notes and later write myself a report, but instead I just kept the idea of research in my mind, and thought about how I could be prepared. I found that talking with other gays and lesbians was the most helpful. It was encouraging to hear the successful stories, but it also was discouraging to hear the failures. I collected a lot of information about what is generally good and bad to do, and also had the pleasure of some great conversations. I tried to talk with a wide range of people to get different perspectives, so I sometimes had to force myself to talk to complete strangers. Of course, this was also a great excuse to meet people.

I also found some good information in books, but had some difficulties with libraries. I did not find many books on homosexuality, and those few did not have much information that was applicable. I was also reluctant at the time to walk up to the check-out with gay books, so I often hid in dark corners to read them. In the long run, the most helpful books I found were those that I borrowed from friends, and gay and lesbian organizations.

The very most important thing for me about coming out was knowing that I was ready to do it. Before I came out to anyone, I wanted to feel one hundred per cent comfortable and content with my gayness, and experienced enough to know what I was talking about. From talking with other gays and lesbians I learned that I would probably need to do a lot of defending and explaining, so I planned on being prepared. This was something very important that I was doing for myself and I wanted to do the best job possible. It was only when I reached that point that I felt I was ready to come out.

The first people I came out to were close friends. That seemed to be the safest place to start, since I felt that a truly good friend would not let it get in the way of the friendship. However, it was still scary as all hell. I was about as paranoid as I've ever been — imagining all sorts of horrible results, but as it turned out, things worked very well and there was no real change in any of the friendships. Sometimes good friends turn out to be not so good. I consider myself lucky since all my close friends were understanding and dealt with the subject maturely.

Telling the first person was the hardest, since I had no idea what it was going to be like. I had decided that I was going to tell my three best friends, and I decided on the order I was going to do it in, and then set a "due date" for myself. I ended up haunting myself with the due date for about two weeks before I finally told the first friend. I kept waiting for the perfect moment, but there was always something wrong. Eventually I realized that the perfect moment was not going to come, so I settled for a reasonably good one. Finally I pushed myself to say "Guess what, I'm gay!" Somehow I got away with it. We talked about being gay, and then about life in general and everything went smoothly. When it was all over I felt amazingly good about myself for forcing myself to do it — it was well worth it. Each time afterwards became increasingly easier and easier, until it became the time to tell my parents.

I knew that telling my parents would not be easy. If everything goes wrong when you tell a friend, you can always just walk away from it, but with your parents it becomes a great deal harder, and there is a lot more to risk. Even though I know my parents well, I still wasn't sure how they would react. From my experience with coming out to friends I knew that anything can happen, and with parents this is even more true because of their being your parents and also because of the age difference. I knew that I needed to be prepared for anything, since their response could have ranged from complete hysterics to casual acceptance to even happiness. It was not easy being prepared for such a range, but when I finally felt like I could handle the situation, a battleship could have fallen from the sky and I would have known what to do.

As well as I could, I set the situation to my advantage. I made sure that I had hours, if necessary, to talk it over, and I also made sure that my father or mother and I would be alone, so they could be honest and comfortable and not have to worry about an audience.

Things went smoother than I expected. I had expected hysterics from my mother and worse from my father, but both responded calmly. They asked quite a few questions, and at times tried to describe my "dark future" (based on their knowledge of stereotypes and limited personal experience), but overall they were very understanding. It seems like the calm reaction resulted mostly from my calmly·telling them. Had I told them during a fight or in some other negative way it more than likely would have resulted in a bad response.

Once I passed the difficult part of saying "I'm gay," it became fun and at times funny. Hearing things like "What did I do that made you gay?" or "Are you sure you're gay?" made it very difficult not to laugh since it pointed out just how little my parents really knew about the subject. It seemed very ironic to me that *I* had all the experience and *they* were asking all the questions. However, this irony also presented a problem. Parents are used to having all the experience and knowledge, so it is difficult for them to believe that you really know what you are doing. Sometimes it takes a lot of patience on my part to deal with the frustration and keep things running smoothly.

My parents always surprise me whenever the subject of homosexuality comes up. Sometimes it's a good suprise, sometimes not so good. There have been times when I've sat with them and talked positively about my gayness for hours, and there are times when they refuse to talk about it at all. I've noticed that over a period of time their attitude goes in and out (of the closet) like waves on the beach. I keep wishing that they will adjust overnight, which is ridiculous considering how long it took me to adjust. But they are progressing, and I find that encouraging.

Probably the most annoying aspect of my parents' attitude is that they keep hoping that I will become straight, despite my telling them that the chances of that are about the same as the chances of them becoming gay. I think I would have to be a saint to always be patient when I hear them say something about "growing out of it" or "not meeting the right girl," but I have learned that they are only doing it because they are concerned and love me. They can't completely believe that I can be happy and gay (sorry about the pun) at the same time, so they hope I'll go straight so I "can have a happy life." I can only be patient, remind them that I am happy, and continue to guide them in the right direction.

In retrospect, I'm very glad that I came out both to my friends and family. There have been difficulties, and it was definitely a risk, but the resulting rewards and freedom made it worth all the planning and waiting. Now my life is in the world, and only my clothes are in the closet.

5 Kozie, ♀, 18, Concord, California

I'm eighteen years old and gay. I've always liked looking at girls, but I never told anyone because I hoped I would grow out of it. When I was about thirteen, around when *Charlie's Angels* came out, I fell in love with Kate Jackson. I thought I'd grow out of it. I didn't; my gay feelings keep getting stronger and stronger.

The first real gay person I ever knew was a friend, Justin. One day he walked up to me and said, "I'm gay." I didn't believe him at first because I've known him for years and he always had lots of girlfriends.

One night Justin asked me to go to *The Rocky Horror Picture Show.* (In case you don't know, lots of gay and "bi" people go there.) I went and it was fun. I started going and getting to know everyone there. One night I went to *Rocky* just a little drunk because we had gone to a party beforehand. I was in the lobby talking to some friends and this girl that I really liked walked in. She came over, said "Hi," and asked if we could talk. I went with her. As we walked into the movie, she said, "How have you been doing?" I said, "Fine, how about you?" At that time we stopped walking and she turned and started kissing me. I started kissing back. A girl that goes to my school saw us and I was scared that she was going to tell people about Jeni and me.

When I went to school on Monday, I thought everyone knew. I was getting strange looks from people in my first period class. When I walked into second period, everyone's eyes were on me. I didn't know what to do. I just stood there for a minute and then I went and sat down. After class we had brunch. I went over to all the friends I hang around with. There were six of them. I came over and five of them just got up and walked away. Only one friend was left sitting there.

"What's going on? All day people have been looking at me and pointing."

"There's a rumor going around that you were seen kissing a girl Friday night."

"So that's it. It didn't take Peggy long to tell the world."

"Well, is it true?"

"Yes, it's true, I'm gay."

"Oh."

"Does it matter?"

"Not in the least."

Out of all straight friends, Diana was the only one who stayed my friend. She started going to see *Rocky* and after a while, she came out to me and now we're lovers.

I am out to all my friends. Mom and Dad know, but they never talk about it — well, at least not around me or Diana. I hang around with gay friends now, because I can be myself around them and show my feelings for Di and no one will look at us and say, "Look at the queers." I still go to *Rocky* because you can be yourself there; not what people say you should be. Also I don't have to sneak to kiss Diana. All week long I act straight at work and at school. But on Friday night, I let it all hang out and party with the woman I love.

6 James Brock, ♂, 24, Seattle

The most difficult problem created by my homosexuality was to deal with the religious beliefs I was raised with. Dealing with these were harder than the years of being called names, the years of being rejected by my peers, and the time spent trying to regain the understanding of my family.

My religious roots are both Pentacostal and Baptist. Either of these alone would have been enough to have caused me severe mental problems, but the two combined, with my homosexuality on top of it all, makes me wonder how I actually *did* manage to make it this far with any feelings for God intact at all!

I accepted most of the rules and ideals set forth by both of these denominations. I taught Bible school, Sunday school, led the singing for both the children's and adult church services. I understood the idea and concept of such practices as "Ye must be born again" and speaking in tongues while in prayer. It was made perfectly clear in both of these churches that:

1. Yes, Homosexuals existed.
2. Homosexuals were damned to eternity in Hell.
3. Homosexuals had no place in society.

Of course I never asked about homosexuality, or even connected what they were talking about with the fact that I was sexually attracted to other males. I always thought of homosexuals as old men who walked poodles on rhinestone leashes and wore make-up. I never thought, dreamed or realized that there were, or ever had been, homosexuals who were my age. Since my first sexual awareness at about age ten, I knew that I was sexually excited by men. Not until about the age of fifteen did I begin to realize that the people I had heard damned time and time again, the people my religious leaders saw as such destroyers of morality, and I, were the same. I was one of them.

It both angered and frightened me. It frightened me as I now thought I was doomed to hell. It angered me because I felt that all of the church work I had done had been done for nothing, and that somehow God had let me down and allowed my soul to be taken by the devil.

I tried to change myself. I prayed every day to have a sexual feeling for girls. I prayed that I would start liking sports. I prayed that I would stop watching sports just so I could look at the guys. But no change ever came.

Religion had been my lifeline, my stronghold, the one thing I was good at. On the ball field I was always the last picked for all of the teams. Then I would proceed to lose the games by dropping the pop-fly/easy-out ball. Not purposely; I just could not get into the spirit of the games. And after years of verbal abuse I had no desire to try and improve my gamesmanship. But in church! I was a whiz at leading the songs, helping with the offerings and communion, teaching. And now I felt that I no longer had anything I was "good" at, and that I was no longer loved and protected by a God I had devoted my life to. My prayers had always been my secret solace, and now I felt I was just talking to the wind.

For over five years, although I still remained as active and involved in my church programs, I was only going through the motions. I still believed in God, but I had no real feeling that God believed in me.

I was twenty before I found the feeling of God's love again. I was just finally accepting my sexuality, and facing the fact that while I was going to Hell, life was still going on. I decided to confide my woes to my best friend. I had grown up with him and trusted him; besides, I could no longer hide my feelings about my sexuality and needed a release. To my utter astonishment, he in turn told me that he also was gay and had been dealing with these same problems of "God rejection." I was more fortunate than most in having this happen to me as my friend was able to introduce me to a very wise and wonderful pastor who opened my eyes, and helped me re-open my heart. Together he and I read the Scriptures which had plagued my life. He pointed out that each of them could be read to say what anyone wanted it to say. He showed me how beliefs differed from religion to religion. And that it was my accepting what man had been saying rather than accepting the feeling of love and peace I had felt before that was causing my pain and feeling of excommunication from God. As he said, I had been given life by God, and these feelings were a part of the Whole Me that God had created. After talking with him I began to realize that I had allowed my life to change and be ruled by mere bigoted ideas and ignorance. I was still the same person I had always been, and God loved me as much then as he did when I was ten. It was such a relief to know that I could be a Christian who was gay, rather than just accepting the fact that I was gay and *trying* to be a Christian.

Religion and religious beliefs can be as strong as the sexual urges facing an adolescent, at least in my case they were. The question of whether or not to have sex is one thing, but the dilemma of wanting a type of sex for which you are told there is no forgiveness by God can be devastating. It is hard enough to deal with the taunting, the jeers, and being ostracized by your peers. But when your religion, the one and only security you have come to know, turns you away, the hollow emptiness cannot be filled in any way.

It is unfortunate that everyone is not as understanding and caring as the person I was able to talk with. It is also unfortunate that by the time most young people discover their own sexuality, be they gay or straight, their religious mores and values are pretty well set in. To someone talking with a young gay person who is confused with the conflicts of their religion and their sexuality, I would first suggest that they convey the fact that they were created and loved by their God before they became aware of their sexuality, and that that has not changed. What has changed are the sexual values and feelings in their lives. They must try to take the time to understand that they, like every other person who has ever lived, must deal with their religious feelings first of all within their own soul. Then, as I mentioned before, they must read their own Scriptures, and find that these can be read in many different ways, and that they must read and apply them to their lives as a person who is first and foremost a Christian, Catholic, Jew, whatever, and *then* as a homosexual. It is in this manner that I regained the spiritual part of my life that I thought was lost forever.

I am hardly a theologian, or a student of the seminary. I am a 24-year-old college student. My lover is 21, and devotion and worship of God has been an important part of our relationship for the past three years. Maybe my ideas and story are meaningless to most, but if they can help even one person to avoid the torment that I faced, then they have accomplished something.

7 Allan, ♂, 16, Gillett, Arkansas

I am sixteen and gay. When I started to come out, I only told one straight girlfriend. Later everyone, including the whole school and town, knew. Many of the boys I knew as friends turned out to be the opposite. They stayed away from me in school and called me "queer," "fag," and "punk." Most of my best friends are girls. I am glad that everyone knows because as the days go by it gets easier.

I didn't realize I was gay until I was in the fifth grade; I am now in the tenth grade. My first experience came when I'd invited a boy my age to our home. We did nothing more than kiss.

When I first told my girlfriend, I hadn't planned on it. We were going to a basketball game and there was this guy on the bus who attracted me so I told her to ask him if I could talk to him. He said nothing, so I never did. I told her because she's very trustworthy and understanding. She wasn't surprised because she knew of a girl who was this way also.

Everyone else found out about me when I wrote a letter to this same boy about a month later. I dropped the letter by mistake, and another boy, who doesn't like me, found it and told everyone. They talked about it around their parents, and it went on and on.

Afterwards, things got so intolerable, I told my best friend that I planned to take pills and I did. She told my brothers and sisters and they told my mother about the pills and also how I had written a letter to a boy. My mother said anyone who likes the same sex is sick. She thought I was mixed up and she sent me to a counselor. I am still going now, each Monday. I guess my mother realizes things won't change and she seems to have accepted it. (My father left home when I was born and died six years later.)

Some good has come of all this. My mother and I seem to have gotten closer. People see me the way I am; I'm more myself than I've ever been in my whole life.

But there have been hard parts, too. After my mother found out I was gay, she let me go to Houston to stay with my brother. I guess she thought it would help me get things off my mind. While I was there, I read in the newspaper about a lady who was gay. She was criticizing prejudiced people, and I wrote her and later got her phone number. She called once, and my brother answered the phone. When he realized what was going on, that I really was this way, he sent me home so his two kids wouldn't be "exposed." I can no longer visit there.

I've lost many of my male friends. Since they know I'm this way, they run off or move quickly if I come near them. I no longer sit with boys in the cafeteria. I sit with girls because they are the only friends I have. To be honest I've had more bad experiences than good in coming out.

From the start it was rough, but I had a caring friend to show me the way. Many times I considered running away and even thought about suicide but then I decided I wasn't going to let other people's criticism run me off or destroy me. There are always going to be people who talk about you or call you names but there is one thing you can do that *will* upset them: ignore them.

I am in a town where I am the only person this way. I would like for you to get some of the youngsters to write, if possible. I hope someone out there will write.

8 Liza, ♀, 17, Los Angeles

I had trouble admitting to myself that I was gay so, for a long time, telling others was out of the question. I had known for quite some time about my sensitive feelings for other girls, but it wasn't until I was seventeen that I first told someone. Somehow, after that, that someone no longer wanted to associate with me. The one thing which annoyed me extremely was that she even turned other friends against me. Unfortunately, ignorance can cause ridiculous behavior.

I live with my father and he hadn't known about my being gay; he wouldn't have even considered it. But he found out over the holidays. He found out through my cousin who is gay himself, but ashamed to admit it. Pretty soon I felt like everyone knew. It was both easy and difficult. Easy, because I didn't have to face telling anyone, and difficult because most of the people around me were very bigoted, especially my father's girlfriend. She made me go see a therapist thinking that I could be "cured." She laid all this crap on me about how gays are all sick in the head. Considering all the years we've known each other, I thought she'd be supportive, but she alienated me for weeks. The tension was really mounting and I was desperately trying to come up with a solution.

Now the one thing I believe is that a person must be true to him or herself, but for my own reasons I had to lie about my being gay. I told her that I was probably just going through a phase. This, you must understand, was to ease the hostility around me. But I knew that it *was* not, and *is* not, a phase.

Since I've been "found out" (I didn't come out), I have been placed under all types of restrictions; no driving the car, not being allowed to see my gay friends, and not being allowed to see my lover. We had to break up, as you can imagine — hesitantly, I might add.

Straights and adults say, "How can teenagers know their own minds, let alone know that they're gay?" Well, that is where they're wrong! It's hard, as I'm sure most of us realize, going to school, being gay, and restraining the feelings we want so much to show. Straight friends can't possibly know and can't even begin to understand the emotional aspects of being gay. As a result, we end up having very few friends at school and our sensitivity about every matter is heightened. There's no escaping the fact that such narrow-minded people exist. The best thing is to build your self-confidence in who and what you are. Avoid those who simply cannot deal with "our" issue.

We all have specific difficulties around being gay. My particular hang-up is how to tell a straight friend that she turns me on. An intimate confrontation like that is such a delicate affair; maybe that's why I have trouble dealing with it.

Another thing I'm sure we've all been through, in some form or another, is people telling us, "You're going to be facing a lot of bigoted people" or "How do you know you're *that way*?" (Most people avoid saying the words "gay," "homosexual," or "lesbian.")

My suggestion would be to start some sort of organization, possibly formed by parents of gays, to hold meetings, dances; maybe a membership club. This could be brought about by pinning up bulletins or posters in areas where teenagers hang out, and even though there will be those who will criticize such promotion, I'm positive that at least one out of every seven would take a glimpse and seriously consider it.

The easiest thing to do is get discouraged, and it won't help any if I tell you not to. Try to recapture how happy your gay feelings make you, and how you enjoy being with other gay friends, who are like you and know how you feel, or remember how it feels to be with your lover. If you haven't had a lover, well then, you have something to look forward to.

If you had friends that you came out to and they discarded you, I guess you realize they weren't friends in the first place. Get involved with other gays your age. It may be hard at first, but you have to make the effort. Take that first step! And don't hesitate to show how you feel, even if you aren't used to it. You'll get used to it, believe me!! All of a sudden criticism and obnoxious remarks will seem trivial to you.

I'll be glad to get in touch with anyone who wants to write me. We may even be starting a gay pen-pal organization!

Publisher's note: We are! See back of book for details.

9 Aaron Fricke, ♂, 19, Cumberland, RI

I cannot remember a day in my life when I did not have sexual feelings. Since the dawn of my memory, not only can I remember being sexually aware but also sexually active to a certain degree. As a child I idolized GI Joe dolls. I would undress them and look at them. When I was 5 or 6 I first became sexually active with my playmates, but I was never the first to initiate anything. What we did seems primitive now but actually it isn't as childish as it seems. We were human beings who had no social inhibitions and were willing to explore our sexuality to its fullest extent. My friends were always boys, and if pressured into giving a reason for my homosexuality this is the only one I can come up with. But I don't think the cause and effect relationship is really that simple.

I managed to avoid contracting venereal disease through all of my toddler and pre-teen years. In fourth grade I had my first confrontation with the Cumberland school system. For some reason I decided to kiss some of my acquaintances in the public schoolyard. Nothing prominent really, just a peck on the cheek. The students immediately ran to the guard on duty, or the teacher, and told of the atrocity that had been perpetrated upon them. The whole thing was sort of a twisted version of the

Georgy Porgy nursery rhyme. The episode was reported to the principal. He held a conference with my mother and told her that her nine-year-old son was a homosexual. I had heard the word "homosexual" before and had a general idea what it meant, but this was the first time I had heard it applied to me. I'll always remember the petrified look on her face when my mother discussed it; it left me with a feeling that the subject was unpleasant.

From early childhood, my sex life continued fervently for years without disruption. When I was twelve I began to detect a sense of guilt from my partners. I felt many times that I got the cold shoulder following sex. It began to spread to other times. Slowly, my friendships with people I had been close to all my life began to dissolve.

This was the beginning of a tumultuous adolescence. Things got worse. I felt isolated, estranged with no one to relate to. I had no literature to read. I knew no one who would tell me that there were books that supported gay rights. I knew of no gay organizations. (There were none in Cumberland, and there still aren't.) My self-esteem plummetted. I found it impossible to confide in anyone about my inner feelings, and that made it all the more difficult to cope with my emotions. Sometimes I would get fearful that someone might uncover my secret. I became paranoid; paranoid not only of other people but of myself and my own feelings. I tried desperately to deny my true thoughts. My entire life was one of utter confusion.

I became withdrawn. I had no means of expression. My school grades dropped and I retreated into a life of non-stop eating and listening to the radio. In seventh grade I weighed 140 pounds; by eleventh grade, I weighed 217½ and spent eleven hours a day listening to the radio. I had trouble dealing with the outside world. And every day I lived in fear that there was nothing else, that I would never know anyone who could understand me and my feelings.

In the eleventh grade I met Paul Guilbert. Paul was open with me about his sexuality almost immediately when we met. I found it an incredible revelation. I had been harboring many feelings inside for years and years and now someone very casually was telling me, "Oh yeah, I'm gay." I wanted to scream and holler and jump up and down but I handled it much more discreetly by saying, "Really... well, even though I'm straight it doesn't bother me." I was very paranoid at the time. Living in a shell for years does that to a person. It took a few weeks before I was able to feel secure enough to trust Paul with the horrible secret I had been concealing for so long. Paul taught me it was not a horrible secret, that it was merely a matter of individuality and nothing more. My feelings about myself soon changed dramatically. I didn't feel any self-pity, I felt anger. I wanted to strangle the entire straight world for making adolescence, which is hard enough for most people anyway, so much harder for people like me. I think I will always carry the scars of the mental vacuum I had been kept in during my teenage years.

Paul introduced me to many of his friends. Most of them were gay, and I found it so fulfilling to be able to share my feelings. I had never expected to be able to talk about those feelings to people who would still treat me as an individual. I no longer had to sit in my room and eat voraciously to lose touch with my feelings. I could share them with someone. There was no secret to be kept anymore. I didn't have to harbor paranoid feelings anymore because there was nothing to fear. It was okay to be gay, okay to be different. And being different didn't mean a life of loneliness and solitude. I learned that my friends and I could be different together. I was not merely out of the closet, I was out of the coffin.

Editor's note: Aaron Fricke went on to make national news in the spring of 1980, when he took Paul Guilbert to his senior prom. He tells his full story in *Reflections of a Rock Lobster: A story about growing up gay*, which was written in the year following his graduation.

10 Jim, ♂, 17, Chicago

I come from a mixed family. That is my father is an extremist —
status symbols, perfection, etc. My mother is a conservative —
stretches the dollar, and is also a perfectionist. This combination
of ideals caused sheer hell when I decided to come out.

It was July, and I had just turned seventeen. I had begun
driving *my* car which I had purchased with *my* money. I already
knew my sexual feelings and had accepted them. So I began to
use my car and fake I.D.s to investigate "my world." I had gone
to a youth group, but the one I went to was full of hustlers and
queens. So I began to go out to bars, porno houses for gays, etc.
Many times I really had to speed home to make my midnight
curfew. My parents assumed that I was dating someone (a girl)
so, at first, they never questioned my going out. But then they got
curious and kept bugging me to tell them why and where I was
going out. This went on constantly, even on our vacation. They
said to tell them and everything would be all right.

Well, it bugs me to hold something back, so the day after we
got back from our vacaton I had a conversation with my Mom.

"Mom, I always hide something when I'm trying to protect you
and Dad. What I mean is, all the times I leave I've been going on
dates with guys because *I'm gay!!*"

"You cannot be gay. . . . you don't even know what it means. Do you actually have sex with these people?"

She did not even wait for my answer. She ran to the phone and called up our parish priest. She got no support; he said that gays do exist, and in fact constitute part of life. This my Mom could not accept. So she called Catholic Charities and made an appointment for a counseling session — for *me*, not her.

I came out on a Monday and the appointment was for a Wednesday. On Tuesday, I was tormented at the dinner table by my parents. My Dad called me every name in the book while my Mom prayed over me, quoting from the Bible. Wednesday came and I was accompanied to Catholic Charities. First, I had a private session and was asked why I was there and what I wanted to accomplish. I said that I wanted to make my parents understand me. Then we had a session with my parents. They weren't there to understand me. They wanted me to go into therapy to be "deprogrammed." But, to their disgrace, Catholic Charities was only interested in how much my Dad could "donate" for each session. Of course this would be calculated according to how much my parents grossed per year.

Wednesday night came and I was at work when I got paged — my Mom was waiting for me because there was a family emergency. I punched out and went to the waiting car.

"What's up?" I asked.

"Just get in the damn car!"

I got into the car and was harassed all the way to our destination. The destination? The office of the principal of my Catholic, all boy, private high school. He is a vowed Brother, which is like being a priest.

First I had a session with him. He said, "Tell me everything. This is just like confession. I won't tell your parents. You have my word." I poured out my story to him. I told him everything — bars, dirty book stores, past lovers, etc. I even told him about the 32-year-old lover that I had at that time. He sounded interested so when he asked me about gay teachers I did not hesitate.

Next he had a session with my parents. Then I was told to come back on Thursday. I went on Thursday because I thought I had a friend, but I soon found out otherwise. I was told how wrong my lifestyle was, and how I was going to be deprogrammed with the help of a shrink he and my parents picked out.

Well, this was too much for me to take, so I asked my lover if I could move in for four days so I could sort things out. That night I packed, made arrangements for a leave at work, and wrote a letter explaining my feelings and how much we needed a break to sort things out.

Friday came and I told my Mom that I was going shopping. I put the letter in the mailbox as I left. At the suggestion of my lover, I called my principal up to let him know that I was all right. Also at the suggestion of my lover, I called my Mom to let her hear my voice and let her know that I was all right. I told my Mom I would call her every day and check in.

On Sunday, when I spoke to my parents, they said they wanted to meet me at midnight in a dark parking lot, *alone*. Well, I did not go because I suspected something.

The fourth day came of my thinking period and when I called, my parents wanted me to meet them at the principal's office. So I agreed and went. When I got there I was told how v-neck shirts, gold neckchains, and Adidas shorts were only worn by gay people. Then I was given the conditons of my return:

1. Give up my lifestyle.
2. Like girls.
3. Give up all past friends.

I pondered these conditions a day and then called and told them that I would be moving in with my lover. A couple of days later I stopped in before work and packed. I said I would be back to pick up my things that weekend. I was stalling because I was still hoping everything would work out.

I decided to give them another try and said I would stay overnight one night. I did not tell them I was testing them. When I arrived after work, Dad escorted me to the garage where I was harassed.

"You fucking queer, you goddamn faggot... Sissy... Do you actually have sex with your lover??"

"I don't think it's any of your business."

Grabbing my throat, Dad shouted, "It *is* my fucking business."

I then explained that this was a trial and since it wasn't

working out I would load my car and leave. They said that would be OK under one condition; that I pull my car into the garage, close the door, load it up, open the door and leave. This was so the neighbors wouldn't see. (I left my aquarium, bike, bird, and a chair because they would not fit into my car.)

When I got to my lover's apartment, we stored everything at his Dad's as we were going to be moving in a couple of days. I still called my Mom every day to let her know how I was doing. The day after we moved, I called my principal and found out that he had traced my phone number and brought my Dad and brother to the old apartment to try to find and capture me. But because we had moved, they hit a dead end.

Everything sort of settled down, so I decided I would go back to school. To my disappointment, I found out my parents were holding my school records up, to screw me. I would have to wait another year, until I was eighteen, before they would be released. I accepted this, and decided that I would go to work full time. I gave my two weeks notice at my old job, but got a surprise before the two week period ended. I was getting off work, and my parents cut me off while I was on my way to my car. "We want to talk," they said. I thought this would all be finally settled so I got into the car.

"We cannot handle you anymore, so you are being committed. As for your lover — he's in jail for contributing to the delinquency of a minor." (This was not true — yet.)

I was driven to Christ Community Hospital where police met me so I wouldn't run away. They told the admitting clerk that I was suicidal and a drug addict. There was no room in the hospital, so I was transferred to Forest Park Institution. And guess who showed up in the ambulance?? My good old principal who, by that time, had told my parents everything that I had told him.

When I got to the hospital everything was taken, except my clothes — so I wouldn't kill myself. Then I was strip-searched and questioned until five in the morning. They let me sleep until seven, and then got me up for a blood test and a regular day with the patients.

I got a passport book in which punches were recorded every

time I did something without a hassle. You could redeem these for cigarettes, or candy, or you could buy status levels with them. When telephone privileges were granted, I phoned a friend of my lover's to let him know where I was. A regular day included group sessions where we would beat tennis rackets on cushions to relieve our anxiety. We also outlined our bodies and drew our features in, played Uno, etc.

During one of these days, I was given some educational tests: the first one consisted of building with blocks; the second, picture interpretation. (What does this ink blotch remind you of?) The third test was for reading comprehension, and the fourth was a math quiz.

The second day of my ten day stay I was sent for a physical where the doctor finger-fucked me. The third day I talked to a lawyer that my lover had gotten for me. Then I signed what's called a "five-day", which was the quickest possible way for me to get out. The doctor had five days to prove before a court that I was insane. If he couldn't, I would be released.

It happened that my parents came to visit on the day my lawyer came to talk to me. They began harassing me and my lawyer as well.

"Is he a fucking faggot, too?" they asked me. They told my lawyer, "You shouldn't represent him; he has no money."

My lawyer explained that money was not his concern at which point my father said, "Oh, then he's your fucking whore."

My lawyer tried to reason with them, but they stormed out saying, "We'll see you in court."

I endured those next days awaiting the doctor's decision. Then, right before I would have gone to court, the doctor dropped my case. Now where to go? My parents did not want me. They did not want me with my lover, and they did not want me with my relatives. Finally I was given a temporary three-week placement with the perfect family: Catholic, house in the suburbs, station wagon, two kids, etc. In order for me to get out, my parents had to sign a release. They let me sit though Labor Day weekend before coming to do it. Then I was released to my new family — after ten days of confinement.

The family was really kind to me, but after one week I decided

I did not like the idea of being pushed from home to home. I went to my Mom and told her I was moving in with my lover again. (I picked up my bird and the aquarium. They had changed the locks on the house, and my Mom waited until I left before going to a scheduled engagement.)

I moved in with my lover and got a full-time job. My records were still being held up so I planned to finish high school when I turned eighteen. All I needed were two more credits.

I had a seventeen-year-old friend who knew my Mom. During this time he landed in the hospital with bleeding ulcers. Mom called his mother and told her about me, saying that my being gay was the cause of his illness. My friend rejected me for a time, but it all worked out.

I gave my Mom my phone number and PO Box number. Then I began getting mass cards and religious articles. I disregarded them, just as I had disregarded the copies of the Ten Commandments I had found in my clothing with "Thou shalt honor thy father and mother" and "Thou shalt not commit adultery" underlined. An example of what I received was a pamphlet from an unfortunate men's home in Wisconsin. My Mom added to the pamphlet, "Jim, if you are too ashamed to come home, go to the Blessed Mother."

There were private detectives following me around. One even came up to me and told me that I should listen to my parents. The others silently followed me, or cruised me, and laughed hysterically when they got my attention. But I disregarded them because I was so emotionally broken down I didn't think my parents would bother me any more.

Then on Friday, the thirteenth of October, private investigators picked up my lover and came to the apartment, where I was, and tore it apart. My parents had told them we were running a drug and porno ring. All they found was my asthma medication and bay leaves. My lover and I were hauled down to the station. I was interrogated alone and then in front of my lover. Finally I was turned over to my parents and charges were pressed against my lover. I was to live with my parents for two weeks, until my court date. I left the station with my parents, but when I got into the car, I was held down and beat up until my face was a pool of blood. I couldn't get out of the car so I had to endure this until we got to my house. (I was told in the car I had to give up my possessions and would be readmitted on Monday to another mental institution.) As soon as we got out of the car, I fled to the police station — still bloody. I filed a battery report against my Dad, but found out it could not be enforced because he beat me in Chicago and we were now in Oak Forest.

The police called my parents assuring me nothing else could happen. When my parents came everything went well until I asked to phone my lawyer. My Dad went into a rage. The police saw what I had been going through and would not release me to my parents. So my lawyer drove all the way out at two in the morning to pick me up. He was assigned as my guardian until the court date. I had to live with a friend because I was banned from my apartment. During this time my parents went through two lawyers and bugged the police so much that they offered to testify in my behalf.

The first court date came and was continued. On the second one, I was put on supervision. It was determined that I could live where and with whomever I wanted to. My parents never showed up at my lover's court dates so the charges were dropped.

I began to make contact with my other relatives only to find that my parents had told them their side of the story. They had done such a good job that most of my relatives wouldn't talk to me.

In February I got my bike and my chair. I had had a silver dollar collection worth over one thousand dollars, but my parents sold it to pay for their bills. My supervision was terminated because I was back at school and still had my full-time job.

Here it is, one month before my eighteenth birthday, and everything is still going full steam. I had visited one of my aunts and my grandmother to show them that I was still the same person. So one weekend I decided to surprise my grandparents and went for a visit bringing my new lover with me. It just so happened that my two aunts came up with their families, too. The first two days went extremely well, but then my uncle threatened to leave if my grandparents did not get rid of the two queers. So my grandparents told me it was all right if I visited them alone, but they did not want to meet any of my friends. They had talked to a Catholic priest who told them the "demon" works through gay people.

My grandma had a civil conversation with my lover before we left, then twisted the story when she talked to my Mom. The next thing I know I get this letter from my Mom:

Dear Son,

I feel I must warn you. They are programming you for suicide. Your lover told your grandma that if we (the family) do not accept you, you would take your life.

Jim, if you are happy with your lover, why do you look for acceptance? I'll tell you why. Because you and your lover do not have true love. You have selfish love and sympathy for one another. You will never be happy being a homosexual and you proved it. You are living like an animal; going from one to another. What ever happened to ---, ---, and who knows how many more?

You wanted independence. What happened? You have your freedom and you still come back to the family.

God help you because you cannot help yourself. They are controlling your life.

Love, Mom

I am grateful that I have such a caring person as my lover. It gives me the courage to cope with things like this letter. I used to let it bother me, but I looked at everything that I have and realized how lucky I am. I am proud of my accomplishments and that is all that matters to me.

11 Sue Cline, ♀, 17, Chicago, and Diane Rodriguez, ♀, 18, Chicago

(Sue and Diane have now been lovers for three years.)

Sue: I'm a senior at St. Scholastica High School in Chicago. I'm seventeen years old and I am gay. Being gay is something I never really thought about until I was thirteen. All along I had had feelings for women, but I never really put a name to it.

I was thirteen and a freshman when I met my first lover, Carla. Before we were lovers, we were really close friends. After a few months, the relationship began to get physical. It was about then that I thought seriously about being gay. It wasn't until my sophomore year that I finally decided for sure that I was gay.

Socially, both my parents and classmates expected me to date. I had a few boyfriends who were straight, but I knew one or two gay guys and we covered for each other.

Being gay at an all-girl Catholic school is really hard. It is even harder when your lover goes to school with you, and you can't do anything, because the slightest sign of affection labels you for four years of school. At first, only one of our friends knew we were lovers. She took it really well, and unlike some of our friends later, always stood by us. Because Carla and I were so close, many people at school immediately guessed. That was really hard, because people can be cruel when they don't understand. Some people just didn't talk to us. It got easier after Carla and I broke up junior year, because then I started dating people outside of school.

I am a senior now, in the midst of a wonderful relationship with another girl that I met at school. We both love each other, but it took us a long time to get where we are now. When I first met her, I practically fell head over heels in love with her. She didn't really seem to care much about anything, even her friends, so I decided to get to know her.

My relationship with Carla was almost over because she had met a boy. Diane and I got really close, even though our friends did not approve. She felt guilty about Carla though, and it wasn't until just before she graduated that I told her that I loved her. When she hugged me and told me that she loved me too, it was the happiest moment of my life. Since then, we've really gotten to know each other, and we're now planning to spend the rest of our lives together.

Neither of our families know about us, but someday we hope to move in together and tell them. A lot of our friends know; they accept us for what we are, and don't hassle us. I love being with her, and I like watching her. She has taught me a great deal about myself. I used to be so sick of my life and my world, but now she has changed my whole outlook on life. To me, she makes every day worth living and special when we are together. I love her in a very special way, one which I've never felt before. It's wonderful to be gay!

Being gay was always something I just accepted. I never felt guilty about it, and never would have hidden it if not for pressure from society. When I was a sophomore, I wandered into a gay youth group called Horizons, where I got to meet a lot of people my age who knew just where I was coming from. Later, after I stopped going to Horizons, I joined the Metropolitan Community Church (MCC), which is nondenominational and mostly gay. MCC did a lot of good for me because I met slightly older people, eighteen and up, who were out on their own. Since I was sixteen, I've become very open, telling a few more close friends.

Probably my favorite part of being gay is being open enough to tell my friends, and walk out in public with Diane holding hands or kissing. I've become involved in several lesbian and women's groups and coffeehouses, and have grown a lot from them. Most of the people I've told knew already — but it isn't until they see Diane and me together that it really hits them. Thankfully, most of my close friends took it well enough that I didn't lose them.

I haven't told my parents that I'm gay yet, and probably won't for quite a while either. I don't think they would understand. In fact, I should say I know that they wouldn't. They knew about Carla and me, and they thoroughly disapproved. So until I'm of age, I won't tell them.

I guess what I'd like to say most to the people who read this book is that if you're gay, be proud of yourself, because it isn't wrong or bad. Also, try and find a way to contact the gay community through rap groups, community centers, bookstores, or newspapers.

Diane: When I was little, I always thought I would get married, have children, and stay home cooking, cleaning and doing all the things housewives do. I expected such a future until I turned fifteen and started dating. I began to see that there were other things to do. I also began to notice homosexual couples and how happy they seemed. I really envied them and wondered why people didn't like them.

I went to a Catholic high school where they actually said being a homosexual was a terrible sin. I had always been told that it was wrong and dirty, and that homosexuals were perverted and disgusting. I never believed it was wrong or dirty, but I never thought I might be, or have the potential to be, gay. All I knew was that I envied them and wished I could be as sure of myself as they seemed to be of themselves.

When I was sixteen I met a boy named Peter, who became my boyfriend soon after we met. I had had a few boyfriends before, none of whom lasted more than two months. I broke up with them because I wasn't happy and I was looking for someone better than the last. I thought Peter was the one. Suddenly I had more friends because I had such a good-looking boyfriend. Everyone liked him and I was invited to a lot of parties. I thought

I had found what was missing in my life. But after a few months, I began to feel uncomfortable around him. I cringed whenever he touched me. He pushed me too far and I lost my self-respect, self-confidence, and self-esteem. I broke up with him and withdrew into myself and became very depressed.

I did a lot of serious thinking about my feelings and my life. I knew I didn't want any more boyfriends and that I felt more comfortable around girls. I didn't go out looking for anyone. I just decided to wait and see who I'd meet and let things happen. After having decided that having a relationship with a woman was what I wanted, I felt much better and I didn't feel it was wrong. Society's preaching couldn't change my mind or make me feel bad about it.

A few months later I met Sue. I fell in love with her and felt wonderful. I had never felt that way about a boy. I am eighteen now, and it has been over a year since I met her and almost a year that we've been lovers. I have never been happier and I have finally found what I had been missing. Sue has helped me regain my self-respect. We have never once thought we are immoral or sinful. I often wonder how people can say it is wrong if they have never tried it.

Being in love is hard to hide, so I decided to tell two of my good friends. We had been friends for four years and I didn't think it would make a big difference in our friendship. At first, they weren't upset and accepted it. After a couple of weeks they said we couldn't be friends anymore because they didn't like Sue, they thought it was wrong, and absolutely would not accept it. I was very hurt and afraid to tell anyone else for fear of losing more friends. Then I realized that if my friends couldn't accept me, they weren't worth having as friends. I feel good about myself and that's all that matters to me.

At first I was a little uncomfortable holding Sue's hand in public, or having her arm around me even in gay neighborhoods. Now I feel more comfortable. Even though more people are coming out of the closet, some people are still shocked when they see us. A lot of people were surprised when I told them I was gay because I don't "look like a lesbian." They don't believe I am gay, just because I don't fit the stereotype.

When I first came out, I didn't know many gay people. Sue and I went to Gay Horizons Youth Group where we met people our age. Since then I have met many people, some younger, some older. I like most of the people I have met, but there are a few I don't like at all. Sue introduced me to two older women that were an example of the typical butch lesbian stereotype. All they were interested in was how fast and how young they could get girls into bed. We went to a lesbian bar a couple of times. The general impression I got was that most older lesbians were only interested in sex. I honestly do not like the bars and the women in them.

Two months ago I started working at a graphic design firm owned by two women. They are lovers and are very serious about their work. They are sweet and very nice and totally different from the impression I had of older lesbians. I am sure a lot of straight people have the same impression I had, which only makes them misunderstand and dislike gay people even more. They should be made aware that we do not all fit the stereotypes.

I didn't expect a lot of straight people to accept me, but I was really surprised when I realized some of Sue's gay friends didn't accept me. They hardly believe we are still together a year later. They don't believe I am a lesbian because I have had boyfriends and didn't have a homosexual experience until I was seventeen instead of twelve or fourteen like they did. They think I am using Sue; that this is just a phase I'm going through. At first it really bothered me that they felt this way, but there is nothing I can do to change the way they feel.

Believing in yourself and accepting yourself is very important. No one should feel dirty or immoral or be made to believe it is wrong. No one should ever feel ashamed of something so wonderful. I am proud of who I am and I love Sue very much. She has taught me a lot about life and helped me through some rough times.

If you love or are attracted to someone, don't deny it, even if you're afraid that you might be gay. Denying it only hurts you. Being gay isn't as terrible as you might think. Once you admit it to yourself, even though it may cause problems with family and friends, you'll be happier and much more comfortable with yourself.

12 David, ♂, 19, Baltimore

Actually, the term "coming out" is more than a bit confusing, because it isn't a single, momentous event, but a series of lengthy stages. Perhaps the most difficult part of this process is realizing and admitting "I am gay." In my case, there was a gradual awareness that I was different from everyone else. Realizing that I was attracted to my own sex didn't lead to feelings of pride and dignity. My first reactions were very negative, which was to be expected considering the pervasive stereotypes.

One particular incident that occurred when I was around fourteen stands out in my memory. My mother and I were watching television when a speaker from a local gay group appeared on one of those half-minute editorial segments that are repeated every so often. After about five seconds, my mother remarked, "I really feel sorry for those people, because they need help. They're really sick!" That just about destroyed the feelings of self-worth I had been working so hard to develop. After a long period of self-hatred, I came to realize that every human being has an inherent beauty. Therefore, some unique beauty existed within myself, and I had a contribution to make to the world.

The next step was to admit to someone else what I had

discovered about myself. Fortunately, I had a very close friend, who virtually dragged it out of me. If it was difficult for me to come to terms with myself, it was nearly as difficult to tell someone else and leave myself open for rejection and harassment. However, when I finally got the nerve to tell my friend that I was gay, the supportive response made all the anxiety in the world worth enduring. I suffered through utter hell in making that decision, but in the end I emerged with a greater sense of self-worth and security. I am still very careful about telling others that I am gay, and have in fact limited this knowledge to a very few close friends whom I know I can trust. There is really no need to tell my parents at this time. Their reaction would be difficult to predict at best.

Although progression through each successive stage makes the next one that much easier, coming out never becomes the simple statement of self-fulfillment that it should be. It is riddled with social pressures and self-doubt. Perhaps the magnitude of each successive step is only understood when you consider that there is no possible way to return to the closet.

Presently I am in the midst of the last stage of coming out, that of becoming active in the gay community. It is both a relief and a terribly frightening experience. Naturally, anyone who is entering unknown territory is going to be frightened at first, but there are a number of ways to approach the matter. I began by becoming as informed about the gay experience as possible through books, films, and other sources. However, I was careful to select materials either done by gays themselves or by sympathetic or non-discriminatory groups. After I felt secure enough with myself, I called the local gay community center to inquire about activities in the area. What I discovered was that there wasn't a lot happening outside the bars, but the person on the phone was extremely kind, and we soon became friends. Now, I am beginning to develop a network of gay friends, so that I can avoid the bar scenes, which I find distasteful. Nonetheless, the bars could have also provided another option for entering the community. What's most important is that you find a community from which you can gain a sense of support and belonging.

Coming out has been a slow but steady process over the last

eight years for me, and yet it seems the road is never ending. Perhaps it is because life is always changing that we must continually adjust. Or maybe we are given a lifetime simply to discover who we really are, and to help others in the same endeavor. At any rate, the struggle with oneself may never end, but it constantly provides a source of pride as we discover those qualities that make us unique and enable us to enrich the lives of those around us.

∾§ §∾

Incest is a taboo topic that almost no one wishes to talk about. Both straights and gays are very uncomfortable when discussing the subject. Nonetheless, there are many silent victims of incest, who ache incessantly from facing a personal tragedy in solitude. The horrors of incest are magnified for the gay victim, especially if s/he was violated by a relative of the same sex. Yet, severe problems occur for *any* incest victim.

In my case, my uncle was the violator. It began at my grandparents' house. I was close to my grandparents and every weekend for five years I had been making overnight visits to see them.

My uncle had just been released from prison for non-support and he was living with my grandparents. He probably could not find any source of sexual gratification. In addition, he had a severe alcoholism problem and homosexual tendencies to which he would not admit.

One evening, when I was in fourth grade, I was visiting them, and my uncle asked if I knew where babies came from. Naturally, I was only partly correct, so he was going to enlighten me. At first, I caught him off-guard, because he wanted to show me pictures of nude women, and I kept hinting that I wanted to see photos of nude men. Don't be misled into thinking that this interest in men gave him incentive. Actually, he severely ridiculed me for showing an interest in men. Contrary to popular belief, my sexual orientation did not make the situation any more pleasant for me. I was silently horrified by his actions. Despite the natural enjoyment of sex, I could nonetheless sense that something was terribly wrong, leaving me with intense guilt feelings. These guilt sensations would only cease years later when I realized that I had nothing to do with these contacts.

I never wanted to go to bed with my uncle, but was caught in an impossible situation. My grandparents had only two bedrooms, so I was forced to sleep with my uncle on the weekends. Besides the problem of having to share a bedroom with my uncle, I was petrified of what he might do if I did not do as he wished. At the time, I did not realize that it was he, not I, who should have feared retaliation. Eventually, I loosened my bond with my grandparents, so as to avoid my uncle, but not hurt my grandparents. By eighth grade, I felt I could completely end visiting my grandparents overnight.

That same year I had to endure an extreme personal crisis. My intense feelings of guilt had built to a climax, and I was beginning to discover other problems that were to come. Among the other difficulties I encountered that year included my first episode of school harassment because of my sexuality. Also, I was beginning to withdraw from people and feared sex even with men who interested me (not that I was sexually active or even wanted to be). Finally, to make matters even worse, I had moved into a new neighborhood, which was quite unlike my formerly protected suburb, and I had problems adjusting. Well, all of these problems ended in five suicide attempts that were cries for help more than they were death wishes. Fortunately, we moved a year later to another protective suburb, where I was able to straighten my thoughts and gain some self-respect. Although I now understand my uncle's actions, I in no way forgive him. Even though I grimace when I think of the times I had sex with him (he was a squalid man, not that it would have made any difference otherwise), I can now effectively deal with my past experiences, and eliminate the hindering grip they had upon my life. In fact, I can even laugh sometimes at the absurdity of the whole ordeal. For example, in twelfth grade, I gave a report on incest to my psycholgy class. Only three students in a class of thirty knew what incest was in 1980! My teacher told me how happy she was that I was going to deal with the topic of incest. She told me, "I'm so glad you're giving a talk on incest, because when I give lectures on subjects like homosexuality and incest, all I can think about is that at least one student in my class is gay or an incest victim or the like. That really scares me." In order to save her sanity, I never told her that her favorite student was both gay and an incest victim!

If you are an incest victim, you probably feel very isolated and alone. Here are a few suggestions:

(1) Try to reason why the violations occured, in order to ease your own feelings of guilt. Frequently, you will find that you were used as a last resort for affection, warmth, or sexual release.

(2) Read books concerning the topic of incest, such as *Father's Days* by Katherine Brady or *Conspiracy of Silence: the Trauma of Incest* by Sandra Butler.

(3) If there is an incest victims' group or clinic where you live, please visit them. However, it is very unlikely that support of any kind will be available in your community, so a psychologist or psychiatrist might be in order. When choosing your therapist, be sure that s/he is very open-minded. After all, a therapist who becomes anxiety-ridden when discussing incest cannot help you very much. Don't assume that a gay therapist will be more open-minded when dealing with incest.

(4) Analyze how this experience has affected your inter-personal relationships. For example, are you withdrawn? Do you avoid all members of one particular sex? Is the past creating sexual difficulties in the present? Hopefully, recognizing the problem will bring you one step closer to solving it.

(5) Finally, always remind yourself that you are a worthwhile person who deserves respect! Leave yourself messages and even write on your mirror that: "I am an attractive person in both personality and appearance."

Just remember that there are others who know your anguish and pain, and wish to ease the sorrow with love, even if we are not there with you.

◆§ §◆

It is truly sad that so many people find life so unbearable that they attempt to destroy themselves; and even sadder that some succeed. The loss of a single human being is a permanent loss to the world of one person's unique perspective, one person's unique talents, one person's future.

Unfortunately, I found myself staring at pills or a knife on more than one occasion as I came out, and nearly succeeded in destroying myself. I vividly remember the long hours of glaring at the mirror, trying to decide if the image I saw was worth saving. At times I would just break down and cry. There seemed no end to my problems. A combination of verbal harassment and physical-sexual assault had driven me terribly close to the brink. No one knew the entire reason for my depression. My parents did not know of the physical-sexual abuse, nor did my assaulter know of my problems at school and at home. The lack of compassion and understanding I was experiencing added to feelings of isolation and entrapment. Following an attempt that nearly killed me, my fifth, I decided to fight back and correct my problems rather than be eaten alive by them. It amazed me how little conviction and effort was needed to make major changes in my environment.

There are a few techniques that I found helpful in recovering from my despair. First of all, set some very accessible short-range goals in order to boost your self-image. For example, achieving better grades was one of my short-range goals. Volunteering to help the poor, needy or handicapped can help because this can instill feelings of self-worth and allows for a reevaluation of the desperation of your own situation. Lastly, leave yourself notes that you are a unique creation offering a valuable contribution to others, and surround yourself with warm, supportive friends.

If you know someone who is going through a crisis, please don't hesitate to offer a friendly ear. Offer support when appropriate, and for God's sake, don't stand idly by and watch a human being self-destruct. Notify a friend or family member of theirs, or suggest professional help to him or her. At any rate, express interest and concern, for each of us is too precious to be lost needlessly, and people need not suffer in isolation and loneliness.

13 Amy, ♀, 16, Texas

I am a sixteen-year-old lesbian. I have been a lesbian since I was twelve. I had known my dance teacher for three years before she brought me out. I was very attracted to her when I first saw her, and from then on, I grew to be more and more in love with her. When I was ten, I had a crush on a friend of my older sister, and some time after that another crush on a cousin of mine. But these didn't last long.

I always wanted to be near my teacher, dance well for her, and have her touch me! Often while falling asleep at night I would think about her holding me in her arms while I'd go to sleep or about her kissing me. I didn't know anything about lesbians then, so I didn't associate my feelings with anything but my love for her.

We became lovers the weekend I was asked to give a special dance presentation in another city. My dance instructor chose me and accompanied me there. She was 23.

After the performance, we returned to our room. She was elated with my reception, and hugged me and told me how good I was. I felt so good being held by her, being so close to her; secure in the arms of a woman I had admired and loved for three years.

Her eyes were so alive, so exciting; her smile so sensuous. When she said, "Let me help you take this off," I could only hope something might happen. I let my arms hang loose as she slipped the leotards over my shoulders, then I cooperated with her so my arms could be freed, leaving the costume hanging at the waist, with my breasts bare.

"You are so pretty," she said, placing her hands on my neck and then running them down my chest, over my breasts and then cupping them in her hands. I loved what she was doing, especially when she licked her index finger and began rubbing my left nipple, making it hard. She did the same with the right one, and I held her tightly around the waist.

"Does this feel good?" she asked.

"Yes, don't stop."

Then she took a nipple in each hand and rolled them between her fingers. At the same time she moved closer to me. From the waist down we were touching; from the waist up, separated enough for her to get her hands on my breasts. Somehow our lips met, tentative at first and then we kissed passionately with her tongue edging its way into my mouth. I began sucking her tongue, and for the first time I felt tingly all over. My next sensation was our deep breathing, then I felt her hands move from my front to my back, and she pressed tighter to me. Then she moved her hands down to my butt, massaging, and pushing my pelvis into hers. When I felt some thrusts of her pelvis against mine, my eyes opened wide. She responded by saying, "You really turn me on... do you like this?"

"Oh, yes."

She said "Let's take this off," referring to the costume still covering my bottom. Down it came, and I stepped out of it. She held me at arms length, saying, "I want to look at you." Her hands moved from my neck, to my shoulders, down over my nipples to my waist; one hand on each side. Then she told me I was sexy and moved her right hand down my stomach and lower. I knew what she was going to do, hoping those sensations I had felt before would be even better. They were, as she concentrated on my clitoris with a circular motion, slipping her middle finger between my lips and occasionally into me.

"I want to make love to you. Let's go to bed."

I didn't want her to stop, but I went anyway. She positioned me on the bed, with my head on a pillow and my legs spread as wide as she could get them. She kicked off her shoes, and leaned over me, kissing me on the mouth. Then she moved down to suck on my nipple. Next she encouraged me to relax and told me that she was going to make me feel very good. She got on the bed, kneeling between my spread legs. Before long she was getting her face closer to me and kissing me; using her mouth and tongue on my clitoris, giving me a feeling I had never felt before. I felt the rush, and hit a climax like I have rarely felt since. It was full of electricity and excitement! Such passion.

We continued that night, all weekend and for almost three years until I had to move with my family. I became a lesbian and a woman that weekend!

My teacher was the first person I can recall who ever used the word lesbian to me. After she brought me out, and I started going over to her house, I noticed books about lesbianism out in the open. I picked one up, and looked through it. She began telling me about lesbianism and people's attitudes towards homosexuals. Until that time, I can't recall ever thinking that what we were doing was unacceptable. For one thing, I always thought that what boys and girls did to each other was bad. Besides that, I thought what we had was special, and since some of the other girls had a crush on my teacher, I wanted her all to myself. So I thought the secrecy and privacy was for that reason; not because others would think it was bad.

I think that finding out that people think homosexuality is bad made me more firm in my desire to stay a lesbian regardless of what would happen to me.

My parents do not know or suspect that I am a lesbian. We are very conservative Baptists, and they would not stand for my being a lesbian at all. My older sister got pregnant when she was seventeen and they went wild! Who knows what they would do with me if they knew.

The only person in my family who knows is my older sister, and she has been wonderful about it. She first suspected about me when I was with my teacher, but I didn't tell her until after we had moved. (She has been very helpful. My teacher swore she would never send a letter to my house for my parents to accidentally find, so my sister receives my mail for me at her address.) I would never tell my parents — at least not before I graduate from college — because they are so religious.... There's no telling what they might do to me. I date guys occasionally, so they will not suspect anything. They don't want me to date much anyway, especially with what happened to my sister, so that keeps the pressure off.

Some of the other girls who were in lessons knew that I was attracted to my dance teacher. I think a couple of them were also attracted to her. After we became lovers, none of my friends knew what was going on. They were a little jealous that I was the teacher's pet, but they thought that was because I was a good dancer. The time we spent together was explained to them, and to my parents, as additional lessons. Dancing lessons, not love lessons!

Since I moved, my teacher and I talk occasionally on the phone, and we write each other. We are not lovers anymore; she has a lover she lives with now. But if we were together, and alone, I know I would want to go to bed with her. We are still very close, though not as close as we were before she moved in with her present lover.

Since my teacher, I have had three lovers including my present lover. The other two relationships occurred just before I was sixteen, and both lasted just a short time. My present lover and I have been together for almost a year. She is the daughter of a family that my parents are close to in church. She is fifteen and will be in ninth grade next year.

Both of the other relationships were with older women. I enjoyed the relationships, but the other women didn't. I really liked them and thought they were very sexy and attractive. But both of them called me a "baby dyke," and couldn't handle having a relationship with me. I think they felt guilty, and felt they were making me do something I didn't want to do — which isn't true. My teacher never called me a baby dyke and never hesitated about me being her lover, even though I was very young.

I guess the feelings I have about being a young lesbian come from being rejected by those two women. But I have also met adult lesbians who are not even interested in being a friend to me. Maybe they are afraid they'll be attracted to me and try to seduce me. Or that I will try to seduce them. Young women have enough problems trying to sort out their sexual feelings, and dealing with their parents and other people who don't like their being a lesbian without adult lesbians giving them hassles about being underage. I am disappointed in lesbians for not caring for us young lesbians. My lover and I are very happy, but we really would like to associate with older lesbians.

14 Mark Maki, ♂, 18, Minnesota

Hi. I would like to tell you something about myself. I am deaf, gay, and eighteen years old. I grew up in a small town and attended Minnesota School for the Deaf. I was seventeen when I first realized that I was gay. It took me five or six years to come to this conclusion.

Last summer, I decided to confess to my mother that I was a homosexual. She told me that I should go to see a psychologist, and I did. I think she wanted to cure me of my homosexuality but it didn't work. My mother and I struggled all year. She seems to be starting to accept me. I hope she will understand my gayness some day.

At school, the boys and girls teased me and called me "Fag." They said, "You ought to get married to a man" and laughed at me. I was angry and hurt.

One Sunday, I went to the Lutheran Church for the deaf. After the service was over, I decided to talk to the pastor and I told her I was gay. She understood, and told me about this lesbian couple she knew. She wanted me to meet them, and gave me their address.

They have made me very happy. They talked to me about how

the pastor accepted me even though I was gay. They said that many pastors make gays feel bad and guilty. I then prayed to God to accept me as a gay person. I found out that God does accept and love me as his child.

Anyway, the lesbian couple invited me to visit them for a week. They showed me the gay places in Minneapolis. Now I am at St. Mary's Junior College in Minneapolis and am very excited to have gay friends. I would like to have a lover some day.

I believe the handicapped may be gay, too. I have several deaf, gay friends now and they are very special to me. Good luck my friends. Take care, and may God bless us as His children.

15 D.B., ♂, 15, New York City

I'm fifteen years old, and I came out to my mother last fall. She was really puzzled about homosexuality and she would talk about it like it was some kind of disease. Unfortunately things at home got worse and every now and then I wound up not going to school, but instead hanging out with a few other young gays.

In October, I moved out of my house to live with a very nice couple that I worked for. I had to run away for a whole week in order to be able to get my mother's permission to move out. My new home was only a block away and I would come home every day to be with my older sister, who didn't know I was gay, and to pick up my mail. I lived there for about two months. During those two months, I secretly dropped out of school. I could never get along with the students and some of them thought I was gay. This really bothered me and it was too much to handle at the time.

In December I met this guy Reggie, who was 23. I met him hanging out in the subway station. Then things really started going wrong. He spent the night with me a few times, which was OK, but when I started coming in late to work, I was asked to leave. My boss also gave me a two week notice to start moving my stuff back home. That day I made up my mind; I was no longer going to stay in that neighborhood. I really had a lot of pressure coming down on me from my mother, family, and the few friends that I had left.

So with Reggie's help, I moved my stuff to different locations in New York City. Everything was packed in either bags or boxes. I remember struggling on the bus and the subway to reach my friends' houses. I left just about all of my massive wardrobe at my previous lover's apartment and I didn't go back to get it until two months later.

Anyway, I wound up alternating between Brooklyn and Manhattan, where I lived. Sometimes Reggie and I would have a hard time with our relationship, and lord knows that they were hard times for me especially! I still remember the night I spent the night in a gay movie theatre! Can you imagine paying five dollars just to sleep? Then the next night we slept on the "B" Train between Brooklyn and Manhattan... The only thing I didn't resort to was hustling. I felt that I was worth more than that and that I'd run the risk of getting caught by an undercover cop.

Before I left work, I had saved up about two hundred dollars because I had worked like a dog those last few weeks. Reggie wasted 45 dollars of mine buying shirts for himself. I wasted 60 dollars on this phony agency that was supposed to find us a room. Reggie didn't work any of this time and we were supposed to be living together. I finally broke up with this guy after being taken advantage of and everything else.

Afterwards, I lived with my aunt for about a week in February. I would go to visit my mother just about every day because she wanted to talk to me all of the time. She was trying to get me back home and she wanted me to go with her to family court to do something about the problem. I refused to do this as it might have meant living in a group home. After wasting two months of my life, she finally convinced me to go back home. I spent the night for three nights but I wasn't moving my belongings in fast enough for her. She called the cops and had a warrant out for my arrest. They call it a PINS warrant (Person in Need of Supervision). Anyway I'll never forget it....

I woke up on a Sunday morning and just as I was opening my

eyes, I heard the rattling of keys and in come these two policemen telling me to get up and put my clothes on. In the background my mother was watching and to make a long story short, they took me away in handcuffs. Can you imagine being brought out of your building with handcuffs on?? They took me to the precinct and asked me a few questions and then they told me that since it was Sunday, they would have to send me somewhere to spend the night. I immediately thought of Spofford Juvenile Detention Center in the Bronx. That place is wild! I could get killed!! So I nicely asked the officer if they would try to put me somewhere other than Spofford. I wound up being taken to this place called St. Barnabas House in the Lower East Side of Manhattan. (The other officers immediately started taking orders for lunch since we would be passing by Chinatown.)

When I arrived there I was terrified. But it wasn't as bad as I thought it would be. In fact you could go out until eleven in the evening and the doors were never locked. If you walked out and didn't come back, you'd get arrested again. The next day at court my mother was there, and at first she didn't want me back. Luckily I knew one of the lawyers of the Legal Aid Society and she straightened things out with me and my mother before we went into the court room. The judge didn't want to at first, but he let me go with my mother on probation. I had to meet certain requirements such as going to school, curfew, therapy, and staying at home.

I went back to school and a few days later I stopped going because there was still too much pressure for me to work under. I was always quiet and afraid of what other people might think. But I explained to my mother why I really could not attend school and she understood. So now I don't have to go to school. I got my old job back and I see my social worker once a week. It really helps and you don't have to be crazy to go! Today I am basically a happier person. I guess that bad experiences can really teach you a lot. For better and for worse.

16 Terry, ♂, 19, Salt Lake City

Coming out to my parents is a major step I have yet to accomplish due to one problem. I am the oldest of three sons and the only son able to carry on the family name. The reason — my two younger brothers are both mentally retarded. I don't want to hurt my parents by telling them about me, but at the same time, I'm hurting myself by telling them lies about having a girlfriend and leading a heterosexual life. My close friends, both gay and straight, tell me that my parents already know; they just refuse to admit it and confront me with it.

I'll admit I have given hints to my parents. I told them about the first time I went to a gay disco, and the first gay man I ever met (a promising employer). They didn't really care about the disco, except that they didn't like its location. However, the gay man caused some worry, and my mother told me to tell him that she didn't care who he slept with as long as it wasn't her oldest son. And, she warned, if that were to happen she would disown me and see him put away. My mother also discovered that I had become fond of her *Playgirl* magazines. She never said much to me, but she did start hiding them.

Then, about six months ago, when I was still living at home, I told my parents I wanted to get my ear pierced. Dad said that pierced ears and long hair were for the "hippies"; he disapproved of both. Mom said that when she saw a man with a pierced ear, she automatically thought he was telling the entire world he was "queer as a three dollar bill."

My parents are really quite liberal though. For my high school graduation present, they sent me to San Francisco for a week. They said it would let me grow up. Little did they know that their son did more than just grow up. As soon as possible, I moved away from home. The tension between my parents and me was becoming too great. I was always being lectured on who I went out with, where I went, and what time I was expected to be in. So I moved into an apartment with two gay friends.

To impress my parents, and because I wanted to, I began to make some very noticeable changes in my appearance. I started wearing jeans and more rustic clothing instead of New York designer slacks and silk shirts. And I quit wearing clogs. I also cut my hair very short. This impressed my Dad beyond words. He actually told me I was beginning to look and dress like a real man should. My parents asked why I was making such obvious changes and I told them it was the latest thing. (I could hardly tell them I was trying to look like the men in *Numbers* and *Blueboy* — a real butch look, you might say.)

Every now and then, my folks would ask me how "Rose" was getting along. Rose was supposedly the girl with whom I had lost my virginity, and was steadily dating. I would tell them all was fine and the subject would be dropped.

My relationship with my parents was improving until I had my left ear pierced. Once again Mom lectured me on her three-dollar-queer theories. But I let it go. She filled me in on all the rumors she had heard about men with pierced ears; the left ear meant you were gay, and the right meant you were into heavy drugs, etc. But I told her it didn't matter to me what other people thought. After all, it was *my* ear.

Making a career choice has also been a difficult problem. Both of my parents hate how delicately I act. I can't stand to get my hands dirty and it makes me ill to have to gut a fish. Just picture "Albin" from the movie *La Cage aux Folles*, only thirty years younger, and you have me. I want to be a flight attendant for an airline, but my Mom told me that was a job for women or men who were pansies. But, it's my life and it's my choice.

Lately, my parents have been really quiet about my earring, but they can sense that this situation with their son is not completely over. What do you think? I hate hiding my life from them, but until I'm faced with it, I'm going to remain quiet. But how long can I go on?

◄§ §►

(The following was written one year later)

Telling my parents was probably the most traumatic experience of my life. For the past year I had been living my life to the fullest. I had been out to my close friends for over a year and life was great. Then came a special event. I had been seeing a guy for about four months and we were very close to one another. Then unexpectedly one afternoon he asked me to marry him. He gave me a beautiful ring and before I knew it my life was flashing before my eyes. Within a few weeks we were looking at houses in various neighborhoods. The pressure was really beginning to mount. Finally I could take no more. I had one major problem in the back of my mind. My parents did not know I was gay. News of me marrying another man would kill them. So I backed out, returned the ring and made a commitment to wait until my parents knew. This hurt me and my fiance. Waiting would be an eternity.

The next step: telling my parents. Mom and Dad are very mellow and I usually find talking to them to be easy. Being closest to my mother I waited until the two of us were alone. One thing led to another and I finally came to it. I asked my mother if there had ever been a secret that she had kept from her parents that she wished she had shared with them. I was totally serious. She laughed and replied, "My mother would have died if I told her some of the things I had done!" She wasn't making it easy. Her cute replies and my serious attitude were not mixing.

She then added, "Have you done anything that you are ashamed of?"

"No."

"Then don't let it bother you, what other people think." I then noted we had become very quiet, but I had to continue what I had started.

"What is it you're trying to say?" she asked.

"Do you or Dad have any fear in your lives about me?"

"Only one — that you're *queer!*"

That one word *queer* stabbed me in the heart. I thought I would die; my whole world was crumbling. The next thing I knew I was in tears. I left the house. I had to get away to be by myself. What was I to do next??

I returned to the house a few hours later and my father had since gone out, unaware of what was happening. Mother was waiting for me. She suggested that we go for a drive to talk.

In the car, her first question was, "How could you have sex with another man?" I told her that I didn't ask about her sex life and I didn't think she should ask about mine.

"What do you do to go to bed with them — get stoned or drunk out of your mind?"

I could tell that she could not relate to me on my level. After about three hours of crying and covering the Utah countryside, we returned home. She had suggested that I go to a psychiatrist and that I needed help, but most of all she said she would help any way she could and that she loved me very much.

During the weeks that followed, my mother went to her priest and he told her that no matter what she thought of me, through the eyes of God, I would always be her son. I also told my father. The one phrase that I'll always remember is, "Your mother and I have no further reason to live. I don't know what the hell we have done to deserve the treatment we are getting. Terry, you were our only hope." Mother also said, "You don't know how hard this is for us, to realize that we will never have grand-children."

I feel sad for my parents. Technically, I was their only hope because my two younger brothers are both mentally retarded. What my relatives would think if they knew hurts my father. For as long as he can remember, his younger brother has always been considered the best of the two, and today his brother is a leading church figure and an outstanding figure in the community. His brothers' children are all grown and married with herds of children and my father has three sons, who he loves dearly, but whom he will never be able to honestly feel have succeeded.

Time has passed and I have done a lot of thinking. I don't blame my parents for my being gay. I don't blame anyone, because I am proud to say to people, "I'm gay." I have nothing to be ashamed of and can honestly say so. People must live their lives as they want, not as others want.

Do not try to hide or ignore your feelings. If you are gay, be proud, and if you are straight be proud. But most of all make the decision; be one or the other. Living two lives will eventually take its toll on you and on those you love. Remember, it's your life and you are the one who has to be happy.

17 Lisa, ♀, 18, Massachusetts

I am an eighteen-year-old lesbian who recently moved to a small town in Massachusetts from a big city on the east coast. Moving was difficult for me because I had a lot of gay friends and I was involved with a gay youth center. The city where I had lived for eleven years was very liberal and tolerant of gays. Though to most of my friends at school I was in the closet, I felt comfortable about my sexuality because of my girlfriend, gay men friends, and the tolerant community in which I lived.

When I got situated in my new home, I observed a very conservative attitude among the people. In my new school, I found that my peers were all in cliques; people who seemed "different" in any way were social outcasts.

Of course I wanted friends, so I tried to conform. I've always been sort of eccentric in my ways, expressions and mode of dress, so blending in with the crowd became a problem.

Soon, I started denying my sexuality. I got uptight when anyone mentioned gays, and I'd make jokes about lesbians or talk about boys. Pretty soon I was obsessed with making lewd comments about the opposite sex. I got a bad reputation for talking dirty and I felt like a hypocrite. People thought I was a real nymphomaniac. I found myself having sex with boys to prove I wasn't gay. Maybe I was even trying to prove it to myself! I didn't enjoy having sex with boys, although there are some guys I like very much as friends.

I became very confused about my sexuality. I searched for gay places in my area, but found none. The closest place was Boston, forty miles away. I don't drive so getting there was a problem. My parents are also very strict about letting me out of the house.

I'd do anything to meet another lesbian, but it's difficult in a small town where people tend to ridicule us.

I'm sure that there are many of us with the same problem. I hope this letter comforts people in the same situation and lets them know that others share their problem.

I'll be going to college next year. I hear that college is a better place to meet gay people....

Much luck and love,
Lisa

P.S. Remember, you are never alone.

18 Mike Friedman, ♂, 17, St. Paul

My name is Mike Friedman, and I would like to relate a few of the experiences that I have had over the last few months because I think they might be of use to people who are in the same position.

Last summer I finally came to grips with the fact that I was gay. I had been having sex with a man since I was fourteen, but I thought that it was just a phase that I was going through. I thought that I would grow out of it, but I obviously didn't. Last summer I decided that I should stop kidding myself. I was gay, and I should be happy with the way I am.

I started going out to the one gay bar in our town, and ended up spending a lot of my free time there, especially on weekend nights. I found this to be rather boring after a while and stopped going to the bar, except for a couple of times a month.

At the end of August, I left home in Illinois to go to a small, Catholic liberal arts school in St. Paul. I had thought many times about coming out to a couple of my straight friends, Brian and Richard. But I was afraid they wouldn't handle it well, and after some thought, I wasn't sure I was comfortable enough with it myself to tell someone else who was straight.

The attitude of the school administration is that there are no gay students at St. Thomas. The President of the school, a priest, has been quoted as saying this in public, and the students treat gay people badly. "Fag" jokes are rampant, especially among the males. A friend of mine used to go to St. Thomas. He was in the seminary, and is now studying to be an MCC minister. He once said, "I've often wondered how many guys go back to their dorm at night and cry in the pillow because their roomate is a hunk." Amen.

I ended up living off campus and spending a very lonely fall semester. It seemed like I had no one to talk to. My roommate was straight and fourteen years older than me, so we really didn't have much in common. At the beginning of December, I decided it was time to come out to my straight friends.

Richard goes to school in Boston. Knowing that I would see him at Christmas, I wrote him a letter and in the letter I came out to him. I didn't really know how he would react but I thought of him as a rather liberal person in general.

I got home for Christmas, and found out that he would not be home until the third week in January and I hadn't yet heard from him. He is not a very good letter writer, so I didn't think a whole lot about it. The day he arrived in town, I spent some time with him, but he didn't bring it up, and I really didn't know how to. He was in town for only three days before he was supposed to leave for Boston. So, the night before he was supposed to leave, we went out and had some pizza and beer, and went to a movie afterward. After the movie, my sister and Richard and I were sitting around talking and I finally brought it up. I asked him if he'd gotten the letter I had sent him. He said yes, and I asked him if there were any questions he wanted to ask me about it.

The three of us sat around and talked for two and a half hours about it. He was very supportive, and told me that he admired my guts for telling him in a letter, not knowing how he'd react. All in all it was a very good experience for both of us. He even told me that someone had tried to pick him up on the beach in Hawaii, where he'd been just before coming home.

He told me that someone had been near him all day, and kept looking over at him all day. I told him, "You were being cruised."

"What?"

"You were being cruised."

I just laughed. Richard did not think it was as funny as I did. I told him he should be flattered. He admitted to me that he was, but wasn't interested. The guy had even asked him to go out with him that night. Richard went, but only after telling the guy he wasn't interested. I still think back on him telling me that, and laugh. I will admit that I don't blame the man — Richard is quite attractive.

Some things that I think you should remember when you come out to a friend who is straight (or at least who you think is straight) is to tell them, and then get them to talk about it. There are a lot of misconceptions that straight people have about gays. Even so called "liberated" people still have these misconceptions. If they react in an adverse way, try to explain to them that it doesn't change you in any way. You're not a different person just because you are gay. Then tell them that it really is no business of theirs who you go to bed with, but that you wanted to share with them an important part of your life because they are your friend.

First and foremost remember that you are an individual; unique, different from everyone else. Being gay is a good thing. Don't let anyone tell you that it is a sin to simply be yourself. No one chooses to be gay, it is just the way we are.

"Take it easy, take it easy." — The Eagles

"Imagine all the people living life in peace. . . ." — John Lennon

19 Kimba Hunter, ♀, 18, Alberta, Canada

I had a label for my feelings when I was thirteen, but it wasn't until I was sixteen that I came out. First I told a male friend of mine. I really don't remember how the subject came up. I was in an institution with him at the time. Ater we got out, we lost contact for a time. When we got back in touch, we started to talk about being gay. He was gay too. I finally got to a point where I said I would go to GATE (Gay Alliance Towards Equality).

Several times I turned around and wasn't going to go through with it. I was terrified! I didn't know what to expect. The most I knew about being gay was from when my Mom had spoken of a couple of gay women she knew, and I got to thinking of them as women dressed like tough men who would beat you up if you looked at them the wrong way.

When I finally got to GATE, I stood outside the door for ten or fifteen minutes, ready to run. Once I got in there, I studied the other people. It's a Friday I will never forget. The men didn't look like escapees from a dancing school and the women were friendly. These were normal people! Maybe I belonged here after all. The next time I went, a woman counselor took me into the office and explained what GATE was. She asked me how I knew that I was gay and a few other questions.

Soon after that, I started going regularly to GATE, and I had to ask my group home parents if I could stay out until eleven. They asked why but I refused to tell them. A couple of days later I was on the phone to my friend and I told him that they wanted to know where I was going so much. He was afraid they were going to give me a hassle. But he said he would tell them where I had been going. So when one of them came into the kitchen, where the phone was, I asked if she wanted to know where I had been going. She said yes, so shaking like crazy, I told her, "GATE." She asked what GATE was and I handed her the phone. She asked my friend but all he told her was that it was a break in a fence that swung open so you could get to the other side. She did eventually find out what GATE was. I was lucky because for the next three months that they were my house parents, she and her husband gave me acceptance and support.

After I had been going to GATE for a while, I started to come out to other people as well. I got letters from friends I wrote to saying that I would never truly be happy with another woman; that being gay was wrong and bad. It was hard to get this reaction to my happiness at finding others like me and at understanding myself better. I was warned but didn't really understand how much it could hurt.

I had been out for four months and my grandmother on my Dad's side of the family died. I went down south to be with my Dad. My cousin came up for the funeral. I had told her I was gay, trying to share my happiness and hoping she would understand. She didn't. We were in my Dad's car when we had a chance to talk. She sat on one side and I was on the other. She said she refused to hug me and didn't want to touch me any more for fear of turning me on. I pointed out that she was my cousin, but it didn't matter. I felt hurt and angry. What had I done to deserve this? It is over a year later and she refuses to even write. I have come to terms with it now. It wasn't easy.

My younger brother also wasn't going to talk to me any more because of it. We got in a few arguments and talked some. Now, we get along again. I knew that he had accepted me when he gave me one of his magazines of naked women. My younger sister accepted it and we have had some good talks.

With my Mom, I know it was hard for her to accept. She still says I am running from reality, but she leaves me alone. She went through what I call her "Grandmother" stage. Every time we passed babies' things or baby products, she'd say something about grandchildren and look at me meaningfully. That was hard to handle. I know she wants lots of grandchildren, but I won't be giving her any. The subject still comes up, but it isn't constant now.

My Dad wanted me to fight it. I told him I had tried. I didn't go through a homosexual stage, I went through a heterosexual stage; trying to figure out what was so great about guys sexually. I still don't understand. I guess that, for straights, it is like it is for me when I am with a woman. I also told my Dad I wasn't happy when I tried that. I experimented in whatever ways I thought would make a difference, but it was no go. My closest friends are guys; there is caring and closeness between us.

When other people find out that I am gay, I have found some accept it and are curious about it. I try to answer their questions as openly and non-defensively as I can. I figure that if they accept me and are willing to try and understand, then I can try to help them understand. I think a lot of the prejudice against gays comes from a lack of understanding.

While I was in the group home, my first three months after coming out were filled with acceptance and support. My next three months were hell! The group home became staffed. I resented the staff because I felt that they were responsible for the group home parents leaving, even though I knew it to be untrue. On top of being upset at the group home parents leaving, there were two staff members who wanted to "help" me. One was going to Bible school to be a minister, the other an avid Christian. I was told that two thousand years ago, I would have been stoned to death. That shook me up a little. At the time, I had next to no understanding of the Bible, nor did I want any. They quoted the Bible to me, told me I would never have true sexual satisfaction, and asked me if I didn't want a man's strong arms around me. I didn't really care if I went to Hell or not; if I had cared, I would have really been in bad shape. But in response to all these Bible quotes, more than a few times I stomped down to GATE. . . mainly out of frustration at being unable to defend myself with other Bible quotes or some other defense on their level so that I'd be left alone. At GATE I found understanding and caring. I still felt miserable but GATE helped a lot. Without the understanding and caring and support of the many staff people I met at GATE, I don't think I could have made it. A lot of times I wanted to give up, but with their help, I found the strength to go on.

After three months, one of the group home staff people I was having trouble with talked to me. From that time we have been friends. Believe it or not, after all that hassle, we are very close and have a deep understanding and trust.

There are some prison inmates that I am writing to who have all helped me in one way or another; helping me to get a thicker skin, or by giving encouragement and understanding. Two are straight but accept me as I am. Another one is straight and thinks I should grow up and face reality. (Gays are against God, hate their parents, and are responsible for all the miserable things in life.) When I read that letter, I ripped it in half. Things like *that* are responsible for all the bad in the world.

The other two prisoners I write to are gay and very supportive. Through writing to them, I hve become more positive, accept myself a lot more, and have discovered that I am OK. I have gotten close to them and they have also helped me to be more understanding so that I don't get mad or hurt so easily when the subject of homosexuality comes up in a negative context.

I hope that I can somehow help others understand gays better, and make it easier for others to come out and think more positively about themselves, because they are special people too.

20 Christi Kissell, ♀, 20, Los Angeles

(Excerpted from an interview by Catherine Stifter, aired on Pacifica Radio KPFK, Los Angeles, June 1981. Pacifica Tape Library, Los Angeles, California)

At the Gay and Lesbian Community Services Center in Los Angeles, we have a number of programs for lesbian and gay youth. We have the lesbian caucus which is a political organization which meets to solidify some of the power of lesbian youth and to start integrating our own political platform into the larger gay and lesbian movement. We also have the regular gay youth rap groups which basically allow for an interchange of our ideas... and from our personal experiences we begin to recognize some of our political issues.

There are a lot of definitions of "youth." I define "youth" as "under 22; 21 and under." Gay and lesbian culture is so bar-oriented that that seems like a good place to start. "Youth" are the ones who don't have the three picture ID's.

When you look at youth, you're looking at school — where there are some real problems with the way that the public schools are set up and the way they handle children. They have a definite heterosexual bias. What they would really like is to turn out a lot of good, middle-class boys and girls who fall in love and get married. Unfortunately that's not the case in the real world.

If sex education is addressed in schools at all, it's addressed as biological reproductive.education. Sexuality is never separated from reproduction... and as a lesbian, I happen to know for a fact that sexuality and reproduction are not integrally linked. What's happening is we're trying to bring sexuality into sociology classes and into psychology classes — to start addressing sexuality the way it is in our real lives. Sex education needs to address homosexuality, bisexuality, masturbation — all the other things besides heterosexual intercourse.

Within the gay and lesbian movement it is important that we integrate young people into positions of leadership, and start to apprentice them in organizing and in using the movement as a forum to push through some of the youth issues.

21   Gretchen Anthony, ♀, 17, NH

I guess my life has always been rough, but the last two years have been the worst, because that's when I began coming out to myself, a few friends, and most recently to my mother.

Nine years ago I had my first big crush. It was on a girl I met in Girl Scout Camp. Her name was Terri F. and she came from another town in New Hampshire. In camp, when we held hands, I guess I must have thought nothing of it. She was the most beautiful girl I had ever seen and I worshipped her. We left camp and up until recently (two years ago), that's all I could remember of her. For eight years I thought of a girl named Terri F.

My grammar school days were otherwise "normal." In eighth grade, I liked a boy named Phillip and eagerly pursued him. But when I was unsuccessful, it was no big deal. My first two years of high school weren't so easy. I'm not very pretty and not one boy in that whole school of 1200 kids liked me. I began picking beautiful girlfriends and writing poems about them. I wasn't really upset that none of the guys liked me. I was pleased that I had so many girl friends and got along with them.

My junior year started and one night at a winter track meet I ran into Terri F. again. I was watching this girl run and I didn't know who she was, but she looked familiar. I asked someone who she was and they said her name was Terri F. I found out a few other things — just to make sure it was her. And this time I really fell in love with her. I watched her at every track meet and got the same funny feeling in my stomach. Sometimes I would walk over near her to see if she remembered me. She would glance at me and then walk away. I looked her up in the phone book and sent her a letter saying who I was. I got no reply. I discovered she worked at a Mall near her town. I started going into the store where she worked. I even talked to her once. Every time I saw her I thought she was more beautiful than before. I still watch her and I know I'm in love with her forever whether she knows me or not.

I figured I must be gay, and I began "liking" other girls — friends of mine. But I made a promise to myself that I would never touch one of my close friends — not while I was in high school. So I repressed these feelings. I began feeling crazy, suicidal, and depressed. I kept thinking that, in such a small town, I must be the only gay person. When I could take it no longer, I started telling friends I knew I could trust.

The first person I told about my gayness was a friend in my French class. She wasn't my best friend or anyone like that; she was just an average friend. But I knew I had to tell someone, because I was going crazy keeping it to myself. We were coming back from a track meet an the University of New Hampshire and I felt I had to tell her then. I don't remember being nervous or anything. I just thought to myself, "Well, if she doesn't like it, I have plenty of other friends to fall back on." So we were riding along and I said, "Nancy, I think I'm gay."

She didn't say anything and I thought for sure that she was going to stop the car and make me walk. She looked at me and asked, "Have you ever been to bed with a girl?" I said, "No, but..." She cut in, "Well, then you're just afraid of guys." And she told me all about her boyfriends, and I just sat there. I never brought it up in front of her again.

When I decided to tell my oldest friend, I was really nervous. We were just walking around and I kept trying to bring it up, but I didn't know how and I was afraid of what she would say. At that point, I couldn't deal with the possibility of rejection. Finally we were on the steps to her house and I said, "Gayle, I think I'm gay." And she said, "I don't believe you."

I said, "Well, you're going to have to because I *know* I'm gay." She didn't say anything and for a very long time we weren't able to talk about it. Sometimes she still says she doesn't believe I'm gay, but now we talk about it and she tries to understand.

After that, I came out to various friends, people I knew I could trust or friends I knew would still be friends. Eleven of my straight friends know and eleven of them have stayed. So far so good.

Telling my friends helped a little but not much, because even though they somewhat accepted it, they did not want to talk about it. They kept saying they didn't believe me.

Then a family with a boy around my age moved into the neighborhood. Telling myself I didn't want to be gay, I decided to give boys another chance. (I'm not always so thrilled about being gay.) Chuck and I became friends and started doing things together, but we weren't sexually attracted to one another. Before I knew it we were both coming out to each other at the Mall where Terri worked!

I told Chuck because I thought he might be gay too, and because sometimes I can't keep my mouth shut about it. We were sitting in this restaurant and I kind of whispered, "I'm queer." And he whispered back, "So am I."

Then I stopped whispering. "Are you really?? Tell me more. Do you know any gays around here? When did you first find out? Have you ever had a lover?"

Chuck has been really great for me because he's my age and I've met some older gays through him. But I still don't know any lesbians and this drives me crazy.

Chuck also brought me up to a gay bar in Ogunquit, Maine where I had a blast. Even if you're underage, you can still get into bars. All it takes is brains and plans. Plan A: Know the person at the door; Plan B: Get there early enough that no one is at the door. I've now been to five different bars, and I've gotten in every time.

One day a Boston newspaper ran an article on gay youth. It

had information about books and bookstores and an organization for gay and lesbian youth called BAGLY (Boston Alliance of Gay and Lesbian Youth). I kept the paper and wrote down all the important stuff and saved it. On my next trip to Boston, I went right to Glad Day Books and spent twenty dollars on books and bought my first copy of Gay Community News.

I finally came out to my mother. She accepted it, but she told me that I have one hell of a life ahead of me. She told me it would be easier if I changed. But I can't change and I don't want to change. I'm seventeen and a half years old and I have yet to meet another lesbian. I have my whole life ahead of me . . . if I don't go crazy.

22   Mark Holmes, ♂, 18, Willow Grove, PA

I had gay feelings very early in life. I can remember wanting to kiss and touch other boys since I was five or six. Other boys would get embarrassed when I tried to kiss them. I never understood what the attraction was, but I learned to accept it. I thought about boys very often, but I also had crushes on girls in second grade. Now I think about boys almost exlcusively.

Although I knew I was "different" very early on, I never talked about it at all until I was eighteen. I was silent about it for at least thirteen years.

The first people I came out to were the people who worked the Gay Switchboard Counselling Service in nearby Philadelphia. The two people I talked to helped me to realize I was not alone. Dottie and Bill gave me a lot on those lonely nights when I called the switchboard. I am deeply thankful that they were there to talk to.

Another big step in my coming out was my first couple of visits to Giovanni's Room, and to the Philadelphia Gay Youth Group. Giovanni's is the biggest gay bookstore in the country and maybe the biggest in the world. The first few times I went there, I went secretly. I soon fell in love with one of the workers there, and became friends with some of the others. I felt very much afraid when I first walked into Giovanni's. I entered the store and knocked over stacks of books. But the people there were friendly and patient. Giovanni's Room has a special place in my heart.

On the first day at the Philadelphia Gay Youth Group, my stomach was a bundle of nerves. I didn't know what to expect. Would these people like me? Would I meet anyone I knew from school? My friend Skip gave me the encouragement I needed and I walked into the smoke-filled room in the Gay Community Center totally afraid, but expecting to have a good time. I did.

I have been going now for five months. The group meets Saturdays from one to three o'clock, and twenty or thirty people come. The group consists of both men and women, blacks and whites. Some topics we have discussed include coming out, straight friends, parents, lesbian mothers, relationships, gay friends, sex, heterosexuality, suicide, transsexuals, self-defense against rape, racism and sexism in the community, the draft, the bars, separatism, and everything else that relates to our lives.

After the support meetings, the group has done club activities such as drama clubs and poetry meetings. In the drama clubs, we act out skits about unusual situations or pretend to be objects. We are planning to publish our poetry in book form. The biggest project now planned is going to the Christopher Street Liberation Day Rally in New York. We also planned an anniversary prom to celebrate our first birthday. As a friend to the Youth Group has said, young gays are "pioneers." We are the future of the gay movement and community.

Although I am out in the community, I have chosen to remain closeted at school. This is not to say that I am not suspected. I have even thought of wearing a T-shirt that says, "I know you know." A friend, Liz, once compared being gay in high school to the experience of wetting your pants in second grade. "Everyone moves away from you." Sometimes the loneliness can be very painful. Many people will not deal with me because I am gay. I know of no other gay people in school; men or lesbians, students or teachers.

But my high school career as token queer will soon be over. I will graduate in three weeks. This will allow me to be more active in the gay community and to establish more relationships. Graduation will also allow me to achieve personal growth. After twelve years of being hassled in school, I will feel a new kind of freedom.

I sometimes wonder how I survived the hostile, macho attitudes against gay people that I've had to deal with five days a week. Despite this, I am learning to be proud about being gay.

❧ ☙

I have recently celebrated the nine month anniversary of my coming out to my parents. I came out to my parents the night after Christmas. I began with, "I have something to tell you." My mother immediately asked, "You mean you're getting married?"

"Well, Mom, not exactly."

Needless to say they were shocked. My mother's first words were, "I don't believe you." My father's reaction was to tell me that I wasn't gay, just confused. He told me that young people are often unsure of their sexual identity, and that lots of kids think they're something that they're not; going through stages and all that.

That night I got to tell my parents many of the things that I had newly found out. I talked to my parents about love, stereotypes, the gay community, relationships, and religion. The main concern of my parents was my safety and well-being. At the time the news was focusing a lot on John Wayne Gacey, the man accused of murdering dozens of teenage boys, and so the case was on my parents' minds. Often the media is guilty of only finding the negative side of anything vaguely involving homosexuality. I tried to teach my parents what most gays were like and that murder and violence were no more a part of gays' lives than straight peoples' lives. I think I succeeded in educating my parents and dispelling some of their fears to a certain extent.

It is interesting to notice how my parents' attitudes have changed since I came out to them, and how I have changed and matured. My mother has grown more supportive of me and less fearful of the gay community. She is growing to be more sensitive to my gay feelings and more accepting of my gay friends. She has even had many friendly phone conversations with my gay friends. For Mom, this is quite an achievement. I understand her intitial fear and apprehension about the unknown world of homosexuals because of her conservative background and upbringing.

Although Mom has grown more supportive of me, my father has grown less so. Dad has adopted a policy of silence concerning my gayness. He has blocked it from his field of vision. Dad now refuses to deal with homosexuality and cannot relate to my sexuality. We haven't talked about it in a long time and maybe never will discuss it again. I understand my Dad's feelings about me and my sexuality. I realize that my father's feelings towards me as a son have not changed. I can imagine why he is homophobic and why he is against gays who are out. For a man of his age and background this is to be expected. I accept his attitudes and I am no longer trying to change him.

23 Rick Cary, ♂, 24, Chapel Hill, NC

Coming out means different things to different people. For me as a gay man, it refers to a long process of self-discovery that led me to realize and celebrate my sexuality. It also refers to my telling others that I'm gay. My coming out process led me to say to myself and others, "I'm gay and proud."

I was a "late bloomer." My sexual awareness dawned more slowly than it did for many folks. During high school I thought certain boys were good looking; I worried about having an erection in the locker room. But I didn't think this was unusual. I figured all boys admired an attractive male body.

I don't think I had heard the word "gay," only "fag." What I had heard about them was negative, and I certainly didn't feel like a pervert. I knew no one who was gay, and no one questioned my assumed heterosexuality. I dated girls and went steady a few times, but I never loved any of them. Still, I didn't think I was different from other guys, until....

One day, while a senior, I was in a shopping mall bookstore and saw a magazine that included a picture of a naked man modeling jewelry. I liked what I saw. Thinking it to be a magazine for men, I bought a copy. Later, to my surprise, I read on the cover that it was "a magazine for women"! I then began to suspect that I was *not* like other boys. Something about me was different; my self-discovery had begun.

I entered college at a major state university as a naive eighteen-year-old from a small southern town. I had yet to meet a homosexual, but that was to change. I met Jerry, a member of a campus gay organization who spoke to my psychology class. Although I cannot remember his words, I do recall his presence. Blond and attractive, he sat on a table's edge, his legs swinging freely as he spoke comfortably about being gay. Being gay no longer seemed unimaginable. He was no stereotype, but flesh and blood. Like me. And I began to wonder: am I gay?

The summer following my freshman year provided an emotional turning point. I worked in a hamburger joint with Pete, a guy from high school. His eyes and smile captivated me, and I recall that he'd occasionally touch my arm and pat my behind. I loved to be with him, and when I returned to college in the fall I thought of him constantly. I was nineteen and had never felt so warmly about anyone. But I never told him I loved him. I couldn't; it was too scary. Yet my love for him added fuel to a fire that was lighting a path toward my sexual awareness.

Throughout college I struggled to understand my sexuality. Was I going through a "homosexual phase"? What did my feelings mean? I struggled to understand the implications of being gay. Was being gay a sign of psychological sickness or immaturity? Was homosexuality a sin? My many questions boiled down to two: Am I gay? Is being gay OK?

I needed help to sort things out. So I read a lot of books on homosexuality from psychological and Christian perspectives. I also talked with a psychologist and several ministers who accepted me. They let me explore my sexual feelings honestly. They supported me as I wrestled to understand not only my sexuality, but myself as a human being.

When I started my senior year, I was still unclear about my sexuality. I had dated women with increasing frequency, but never felt love for any of them. I discovered that I could perform sexually with a woman, but heterosexual experiences were not satisfying emotionally. I felt neither love nor emotional oneness with women. Indeed, I had concluded that I was incapable of human love.

During that year I again experienced love like I had felt for Pete. Stephen was a hall-mate, and I was drawn to him physically and emotionally. I longed to be with him. We teased each other, but I was afraid to tell him of my love. My feelings for Stephen provided more fuel for the fire.

At the age of twenty-one, I looked at the evidence in my life. I realized that the only people I had loved were men, and now I loved Stephen. During college my gay feelings had grown increasingly strong; my sexual fantasies and dreams were about men. Although I had not had sex with a man, I knew how I felt. Through counseling and reading I became able to say "Gay *is* good." I realized that being gay is neither a sickness nor a sin. During my final semester, after four years of conscious struggle, I was able to say, "I am gay and proud."

I went to my first gay dance (was I scared!) and had a wonderful time. Right after graduation I met Stuart. We fell in love, and for the first time I shared love and sex with a man. I felt whole and at peace with myself and with God. Finally I had come to see my sexuality with clarity. I could affirm and celebrate my gayness. I had come out.

My coming out includes telling others I'm gay. Some gays tell everybody, but that's not my style. I have chosen to be selective in telling others. The Bible says, "Do not throw your pearls before swine, lest they trample them under foot and turn to attack you." Well, my gayness is one of my treasured pearls, a pearl I own after paying a great price of personal struggle. I won't share that treasure with everybody. However, I have come out to many folks whom I care about and with whom I have significant relationships.

Most of the non-gay people who know I'm gay are friends. I began coming out to friends while a senior in college. Coming out was scary then... and still is! I never know how someone will react to my gayness. Some friends suspected all along; others were totally suprised. Some said "So what?"; others were upset. I've told several dozen friends and none have rejected me. Oh, many have struggled to understand my gayness, but they were willing to struggle. And my coming out has often led to deeper, more open relationships. I've been fortunate; other gays have experienced more rejection than I have.

Over the years, I've learned a few things about how to come out to someone. I need to tell my friend that I want to share something very personal, something that she or he may not understand at first. I want my friend to know that I desire a deeper friendship. I need to avoid coming out when I'm angry with someone. I want my coming out to be an act of love; the sharing of a treasured pearl with a friend. I also remind myself that an initial reaction of disbelief or anger is common. If my friend is upset, he or she may need time to wrestle with my gayness. I can offer to be there and answer questions (and often there are lots of questions!), but I cannot make my friend accept me. Every time I come out to someone I risk losing that friend. With each individual I decide if I want to take the risk.

Perhaps nothing is riskier than coming out to parents. I came out to my parents at the same time I came out to myself, but I wasn't prepared for their reaction. How I wish I could have read the Switzer's book *Parents of the Homosexual* before I came out to them. I could have had more realistic expectations, for the Switzers described my parents' reactions with amazing accuracy.

Mom and Dad first reacted with disbelief. "You can't be gay! You must be mistaken." They were so upset they sent me back to school and said, "Don't come back home until we say you can." Those were the most painful words I've ever heard. For a brief moment I considered suicide, but I had friends and ministers to turn to for support. I was not alone.

After a few weeks they re-established contact with me. They realized they could not run from the issue. After the initial shock, they felt a flood of emotions. *Anger.* They were angry with me for causing them so much pain and for refusing to see a psychiatrist. They were angry with everyone who might have "made" me gay — college friends, the ministers who counseled me, and finally, themselves. They felt guilty and wondered, "How did we fail?" *Fear.* They knew it's tough being gay in our society, and they feared I was throwing away my college education and promising future. *Sadness.* The "little Ricky" they knew was no longer the same. Their expectations for me, especially a wife and children, were suddenly taken away. Much had changed, and they grieved for the loss of their dreams for my life. . . and their lives too.

That's a lot of heavy emotion, and I felt emotional too. I was angry with them for their reaction. I feared for my future and felt sad that our relationship was strained. The first year was incredibly tense, so tense that it was often terribly uncomfortable for us to be together. We have talked some about my gayness, but we most often avoid the topic. It's scary for all three of us. Yet we *need* to struggle with each other and our relationships. Happily, they have often demonstrated their love for me in recent years. I am still their son, and our lives go on.

Thus far in my life, I have come out selectively, but one day I may decide to come out very publicly as some gays have done. A part of me wants to do that, but for now I choose otherwise. Each gay must make his or her choice. Coming out, to oneself and to others, is an intensely personal and individual experience. Each coming out story is unique. This has been mine, but the story has not ended because I am continually coming out. I will always need to reaffirm the goodness of my gayness and share that pearl with people I care about. I am coming out.

Resources for Parents

Fairchild, Betty and Hayward, Nancy. *Now That You Know: What Every Parent Should Know About Homosexuality.* New York: Harcourt, Brace, Jovanovich, 1979.

Switzer, David K. and Shirley. *Parents of the Homosexual.* Philadelphia: Westminster, 1980.

Parents of Gays, PO Box 553, Lenox Hill Station, New York, NY 10021; 914-793-5198. (This is an international organization for the parents of gays. Many cities have a group or contact person. Write or call for a current resource list.)

Guide to Religious Gay Groups

Affirmation/Gay and Lesbian Mormons, Box 46022, Los Angeles, CA 90046

Affirmation/United Methodists for Lesbian/Gay Concerns, Box 1021, Evanston, IL 60204

Bet Mispocheh, Box 1410, Washington, DC 20013, (202) 833-1638

Beth Chayim Chadashim, 6000 W. Pico Blvd., Los Angeles, CA 90035, (213) 931-7023

Brethren/Mennonite Council for Gay Concerns, Box 24060, Washington, DC 20024

Dignity Inc., 1500 Massachusetts Ave, NW, Suite 11, Washington, DC 20005

Evangelicals Concerned, 30 E. 60th St., New York, NY 10022

Friends for Lesbian/Gay Concerns, Box 222, Sunneytown, PA 18084

Integrity, 10 Mercier Ave., Dorchester, MA 02124

Lutherans Concerned for Gay People, Box 19114A, Los Angeles, CA 90019

New Ways Ministry, 4012 29th St., Mount Rainier, MD 20712, (301) 277-5674

Pentecostal Coalition for Human Rights, Box 386, Howard University, Washington, DC 20059, (202) 387-2858

Presbyterians for Gay Concerns, Box 46412, Los Angeles, CA 90046

S.D.A. Kinship International Inc., Box 1233, Los Angeles, CA 90028

Sh'ar Zahav, Box 5640, San Francisco, CA 94101, (415) 621-2871

Unitarian-Universalist Office of Lesbian and Gay Concerns, 25 Beacon St., Boston, MA 02108, (617) 742-2100

United Church of Christ Coalition for Lesbian/Gay Concerns, Box 1926, San Francisco, CA 94101

United Lesbian and Gay Christian Scientists, Box 7467, 256 S. Robertson, Beverly Hills, CA 90211

Universal Fellowship fo Metropolitan Community Churches, 5300 Santa Monica Blvd, Rm. 304, Los Angeles, CA 90029, (213) 464-5100

24 Deborah, ♀, 18, Los Angeles

My name is Deborah. I'm a senior in a Los Angeles county high school. I am also gay. Although I figured out that I was gay the summer I was sixteen, I didn't admit it to myself for a year and a half. I knew that I wasn't interested in boys when I was sixteen. I was in love with an older female friend who was thirty-six and married. We'd go out as friends but I'd feel *a lot* more for her than she did for me. Once, she caught me spying on her. She asked me if I thought I might be gay. My first reaction was, "Who me? I'm too young to be gay. I'm sure it's only a stage."

Over the months, I realized that it wasn't a stage. I discovered that I had no feelings for boys, and that was all my friends used to talk about. I realized that the subject of boys was boring to me. I knew that I was gay then because I was eighteen and I didn't know one other eighteen-year-old, twelfth grade girl who didn't like boys.

My first gay contacts were made in gay groups of Alcoholics Anonymous, which I belong to. I also joined a lesbian rap group at UCLA. I found out about this through a friend who goes to UCLA. I contacted the Gay Center in Hollywood and am attending a class there. I also made some contacts and met my first lover through an organization called The League, where contact is made by mail.

At first the word "lesbian" sounded negative to me. It was used as a put down by my peers and family. I also was very confused by the stereotypes of lesbians. I used to think that I *had* to wear guy's clothing, but now I know that that was only a stereotype. I realize that it doesn't mean I have to look or dress any particular way.

I tried to come out to my Mom two months ago, but she thinks it is a stage. She tells me, "When I was young, I didn't like boys either; you'll grow out of it." I am an only child, so naturally she has hopes that I'll get married and have grandchildren "for her." I told her that that notion was rather selfish and that there was no law that required me to get married and have children. She often pressures me about guys and I either tell her that she is boring me or I ignore her. Personally, I think she'll accept it when she is ready.

I would like to give some advice on how to tell your friends about being gay. First of all, don't tell just anyone. You have to really trust someone in order to tell them. You must observe a person for a long time to see if they are someone you should tell. It is best not to tell people who are prejudiced, overly religious, or immature. Before telling someone, it is best to find out their general opinion of the subject. The best time to bring it up is when the subject of sex and/or marriage is being discussed. I've basically gotten three reactions:

1) "It's no big deal, just don't try anything on me." (if they are female).

2) "Eeew — Gross!! You're disgusting."

3) "You are a sinner."

All but one person that I've told are still my friends. They don't bring it up, but sometimes we all joke around about it. They don't intend to hurt me, though. Many times, they can't relate to my talking about girls the way they talk about guys. Sometimes it freaks them out, but they are still my friends.

Often I am paranoid in the presence of this guy that I know. I told him and he is not my friend any more. I see him at school, but, so far, nothing has been said.

It really isn't as big a deal as most teenagers make it out to be. On the bus, people are always telling "fag" jokes. I usually ignore them. Not everyone in my life has to know — it is my business and that is what's important.

25 Bill Andriette, ♂, 16, Levittown, NY

As a young child I unquestioningly accepted the popular perception of homosexuals until I discovered that I was one. That realization hit me when I was twelve, though already I had sometimes mulled over the possibility in my mind. It was not that a nascent sexual drive was emerging with my pubic hairs, but rather that I was beginning to analyze and understand the things I had keenly felt and blithely savored since age five or six.

It was a shock to discover that my impassioned, if inarticulated, love affairs with fellow schoolboys which had held so much poignant beauty carried that weighty word *homosexual*. Armed only with the information gleaned from twelve years of living in a homophobic society, I sat with the dictionary opened to that fateful term, smarting still from having made the connection between its meaning and my feelings.

Into the dark confusion of sexual self-discovery, gay culture emerged to me as a guiding light. It not only assured me that there were others of my persuasion, it also gave a structure to what had been a shapeless mass of unsorted desires; it showed me how those desires could be confirmed, developed and ultimately satisfied. The gay media gave me a sense of community that helped take the place of what were often inaccessible gay relationships.

Almost invariably, being gay and young puts one at odds with institutions concerned with youth. The home and school may cease to be sources of emotional support, or at least diminished ones as the young person discovers his or her inability to deal with homosexuality. Such rejection, when it does not have disastrous consequences, is motivation to explore the world beyond. It can propel the rural or suburban gay into the city, make the shy person stand up for his or her rights. It can lead to books that would have been otherwise unread, and politics that would have been left unexplored.

The young gay just coming out needs, above all, accurate information to cut through the ignorance caused by silence. If resourceful, he or she may find information in the public library available more or less anonymously. But the gutsy, down-to-earth reassurance needed will almost never be found amidst the dusty tome the library dared to buy. And what benefit does it bring to know Gay is Good when your peers think Homosexual is Horrible? For gay liberation to have any value for youth, people must be reminded, preferably in fifth or sixth grade sex education classes, that gay is not only good, but probably a part of most sexual makeups.

26 David Johnson, ♂, 17, Wheeling, WV

When I was 15, my brother Troy left home and I inherited his chores and still carried my own. I didn't really mind because my allowance went up from five to ten dollars a week. Christmas vacation had just ended as I recall, and I was returning to school. Mother had said I could get my hair styled any way that I wanted, and I had decided on an afro because I wanted to look like Troy. (I still recall the time I went to school with my hair combed and glasses off and no one knew who I was.) I finally had the money and told Mother I wanted an afro. She hit the roof. I was surprised at the way I reacted because I never really argued with Mother. But suddenly everything that I had stored up — all my frustrations and hatreds — came pouring out at her. She couldn't handle it I guess; she expected it from Troy or Korri . . . but from me, Never!

I stomped into my room and for three solid hours I sat there brooding. Then at about 8:30 she came in very sober (a sure sign that she had been drinking) and I could tell she had been crying. As in the past, on rare occasions, she asked me if I wanted to see if we could reach my father on the phone. We had been trying to for the last ten years and had never been able to reach him, but this night it was different. We got hold of Grandma Davis and she called Dad, and he called us. Mother talked to him first, and then I talked to him.

Before I knew it, arrangements had been made for me to fly to California and stay with him. But first Mother had made him swear out his address and send a two-way plane ticket. She wanted to make sure that once I got there he didn't take me and vanish.

On a Wednesday evening, I found myself at Tampa airport getting ready to board a plane to San Francisco, expecting Mother to call off her bluff. Instead, she called mine. There I was boarding a plane to San Francisco just to keep from losing face. Pride is a terrible thing.

The plane trip lasted for what seemed like years but was only hours. I thought about a lot of things; that I wouldn't see my friends for at least three months and that I wouldn't see my great-grandmother or Mom for a long time. I was giving up what at that moment seemed to be everthing just to see the man who was my blood father — a man whose face I couldn't even remember. I fell asleep feeling upset and wondering what would happen to me. I awoke when the plane landed.

I quietly picked up my briefcase full of *Mr. Marvel* comic books, while listening to the stewardess over the speaker welcoming us to San Francisco. I got off the plane, and thought that through the crowd ahead I could see the man who could be no one else except my father. The resemblance between us was amazing. We started to walk towards each other, and when we met it seemed to be an explosion of love. We shook hands and he expressed how happy he was to see me and took my briefcase. Then he introduced me to a strange woman, Jerry, whom I supposed was my step-mother. We went and picked up my luggage and went to the car.

∽§ ξ∾

One day Dad, Jerry and I were invited over to a friend of Dad's for dinner. She appeared to be quite a nice lady, though I thought she was quite tall for a woman; not at all what I was used to. She kept having me run down to the corner store for odds and ends. On the last run she bent over to get some money out of her purse. Quite by accident, I happened to glance down the front of her dress. There on her chest was all this hair. Realizing that she was a he about caused me to go into a coma. It was the last thing I expected. Maybe all those things Mom had said about Dad were true!

Then about a week later, they had a friend of theirs from work come over to style my hair. His name was Claude. I had met him once before and could tell he was gay. As he was cutting my hair, his crotch kept pushing itself into my shoulder. It was definitely a turn-on, and at that moment I came to the conclusion that I could be nothing but gay. Claude, wherever you are, thank you for that meaningful shove which helped me make up my mind as to who I was and am.

❦ ❧

I recall that I used to put on my tight white jeans and go walking down Polk Street which was widely known as a gay street. I would walk the whole street and come back again looking and hoping somone would notice me and pick me up, but I never had any luck except for once a man asked me if he could walk with me. I answered with a polite "no," and went on my way home, later wondering why and regretting it.

❦ ❧

Finally my days of skipping school caught up with me and Dad received a note asking why I had been missing so much school. Well, Dad tried to have a father-son talk; I must give him credit for that. Only he said a few things I didn't quite care for. He said I wasn't going to come between Jerry and him (which I wasn't trying to do anyway), and that running away wouldn't solve anything.

I never would have thought about leaving, but he had gone and planted the idea in my head. That was the night I decided to become a runaway... a decision that wasn't so smart but I'll never regret it, no, never. The next night I kept arguing with myself whether to do it or not. Finally I took 36 dollars from the desk, hung my keys on the door, and then, with only the clothes on my back and a bag containing my drawings, I walked out the door, which locked behind me. For me, there was no turning back.

It was the first time I had ever been out at night, except for the night I went to the house of Reverend Moon's church and ate dinner there. I walked to the Greyhound bus station, and I purchased a bus ticket for Los Angeles. I picked Los Angeles on pure instinct, and because it was the only place I could go on the money I had.

I boarded the bus at 10:30 p.m. on a Sunday night and it left at 11:00. By this time Dad and Jerry would have discovered that I had left. As I recall, at the second stop after we had left San Francisco, an old man got on and sat down beside me. I was listening to the two guys sitting behind me when he struck up a conversation. He askd me where I was heading and I told him. Then he asked me how old I was and I lied and said I was eighteen. Then we just talked about life... his ending and mine beginning. About an hour before we would hit L.A., he got off the bus. I remember saying to him that I didn't know what would happen to me and he said in an all-knowing voice, "You'll be fine. You're gonna live through a lot of hell, but you'll make it... Just depend on luck." I watched him get off and he faded away into a crowd of faces. I kind of had a feeling that I had just talked to my guardian angel.

We arrived in Los Angeles at 6:00 a.m. and I went to the bus station cafeteria and had some coffee while I smoked some cigarettes. I was in no hurry. After all, I had no place to go. Finally I got up and left. I walked around downtown L.A. for a few hours. Finally I decided to go to Hollywood. I got the 45 Bus and stayed on from one end to the other. By this time I had gotten more than a bit depressed and had decided to end it all by getting a cheap motel room and slicing my wrists. But then, before I got off the bus, I decided to call my father and have him send for me. I caught a bus back to L.A. and went to the Bonaventure Motel. I got five dollars in change, and tried to reach him but no one answered the phone.

I went back outside and wandered around a bit till I came to a church. I went in. It was the most beautiful church I had ever been in. I walked up to the altar and knelt, praying for God to help me.

When I left the church, I returned to the motel. By this time it was about 8:00 and I was a bit hungry and thirsty, so I went to the underground mall across the street and got a coke and hamburger in a little snack shop. I sat and ate. An adorable bus boy came out and started to clean up. When he was through he came over and sat down beside me. He asked my name, and for a while I showed him my drawings. He really liked one, and I said he could have it if he'd let me sleep on his couch. He agreed, and went to check out, taking the drawing with him. He went through two doors and I never saw him again.

It was 10:00 when I went back to the motel. I had decided to sleep in the lobby. I plopped myself down on one of the circular couches, but every time I fell asleep, a guard would wake me up and say, "You can sit here as long as you like, but you can't sleep." By this time I was getting more than a bit frustrated, so I got up and left. I'd take my business elsewhere.

I found myself walking the deserted streets of downtown L.A. at 4:00 the next morning and decided to go back to the motel. This time I sat by the pool. About 6:00 a.m., I went back inside looking for a coffee shop that might be open.

I was walking through a hallway when this gorgeous black security guard came towards me. I said to myself, "David, you're in trouble now," but to my surprise, he asked if he could help me. We ended up in a deep conversation. Finally he asked if I was gay and I said yes. It seems that he was, too.

His name was Jade, and he told me that he lived with his lover, Fred, and they managed an apartment. He said if I needed a place to stay that I could stay with them and I accepted.

We arrived at his apartment at 9:00 a.m. on a Tuesday morning early in March and, as I recall, Fred was asleep on the couch. Jade asked me if I'd like to see some of the vacant apartments. I, being the naive child, said yes.

He led me into the first one which hadn't any furniture and I didn't think it was worth looking at. The second one had a couch, but it hadn't been cleaned yet. He then took me into the walk-in closet and started kissing me. My natural desire for sex was of course taking control of me, but because of my upbringing,I felt it wasn't the right time or place. So I found the words and managed to get myself out of tight spot. Then we went back to their apartment, and I went into their bedroom and fell into a very deep sleep.

I finally told Jade my true age and he took me to the Gay Community Center which was in Hollywood. We talked to a lawyer to see what could be done to insure that no one tried to cart me off somewhere I didn't want to go.

We found out that as long as I didn't break any laws I couldn't be touched and then I was told about a youth rap every Friday night at eight if I would like to meet people my own age. I wasn't too thrilled about this because kids had always made fun of me because of the way I talk.

While waiting to catch the bus Jade told me I would have to be careful every time I came to Hollywood for there were pimps who would grab you off the streets, take you home and rape you, and then have you work the streets for them with no hope of getting away. It painted a very ugly picture in my mind and I promised to be very careful always. Then I cheerfully added, "After all, if I was going to work the streets, I would certainly want my own boss — me!"

The first Friday night after that I didn't go, but throughout the following week Jade and Fred kept saying I should, so I went. I had bought a pair of tight blue jeans and a new shirt Thursday so I wore them, and Jade gave me five dollars and told me to get something to eat, and if it was late to catch a cab back. He said if I rode the bus back after 11:00 p.m. I might get picked up for prostitution. I casually said I'd bring me back a man as I walked out the door, never hearing Jade telling me not to.

I boarded the bus and was there by seven. There was a Jack-in-the-Box right next door so I went in and got something to eat. I took my tray and grabbed a window seat so I could cruise the guys as they walked by. I felt great. I was on my own; or so I thought....

I sat there silently sipping my coke and smoking a cigarette when two beautiful guys walked by. One was kind of short with blondish, long hair. The other was tall, blond and had a good tan. He was wearing ever so tight blue jeans, a tight silk shirt, a leather vest, a studded belt, and had a leather key strap attached to his belt loop. I fell in love. I wished later it had been lust.

I immediately dumped my tray and walked out. I followed this couple right into the Center. Once inside I saw them talking to a girl. I went up and asked if this was the right place for the youth rap. She said yes and introduced herself, and then introduced me to the short guy whose name was Bobby and then to Ray who reached out and shook my hand. I felt electricity surge through my whole body, and then he and Bobby wandered away and started to talk to someone else. For once in my life I wanted somebody so badly I decided to reach out and grab him while I still had the chance.

When the youth rap was to begin, we all entered a room encircled with couches. Bobby and Ray sat down, and I sat down where the next couch began, with only the arms of the two couches between us. The rap sesion began and so did I; on my deliciously evil plan on how to get this hunk for my own purposes. I just didn't know what had gotten into me. I guess it was love. . . .

I withdrew a cigarette and before I could get my matches out, Ray had lit it, and then he lit one of his own. Bobby just smiled and his eyes told me what he was thinking, "Kid, you don't have a chance."

I started chain smoking and Ray kept lighting them as fast as I could get them out. Finally he ran out and I let him smoke mine. When we stopped for a break, both of us had run out of cigarettes. He went out and brought back two packs. He gave me one and I tried to give him money for them but he refused. Again I looked into Bobby's eyes and read his thoughts; "But, then again, maybe you do have a chance, kid."

For another hour Ray lit my cigs and the meeting was coming to an end. He and Bobby were getting ready to leave when I asked Ray if he had a car. He said yes and I said I needed a lift home and could give him a couple of dollars for gas. He said okay and we loaded up into a '72 Vega.

Bobby and I were talking about transvestites, and the conversation was suddenly called to a halt as we pulled up to the gas station. Then when we pulled out Ray started talking to Bobby about leaving Jobcorp and moving into Bobby's place. Bobby didn't like this idea at all because, as he put it, he didn't want to be tied down to anyone.

❧

We went to my place and went in, and this time Fred was home. I asked him if Ray could stay the night; he said yes and then went into the bedroom. He came back with sheets and a small tube of K-Y stuck inside a towel. He also handed me the keys to a vacant apartment.

I took Ray up to the room and we talked for a couple of hours, hours which seemed forever to me, who felt like a bride on her wedding night waiting for her new husband to get out of the john and into the bed. As we talked I started to get excited sexually. Ray slipped his hand over onto my lap, then he gave me a look of genuine surprise. He then apologized for not being "well hung." My lord, when I finally got his clothes off I discovered he was hung like a greek god, and he looked like one in every other aspect also. Needless to say the rest of the night passed over and neither of us got any sleep at all. I was in love. . . .

27 Anonymous, ♂, 16, Toronto, Canada

Hi. I'm 16 and I'm gay. I share a common problem with young gays, and that's finding other gays in school.

There is a new guy in our school who just came from a boys' private school. I think he is cute and would like to get to know him better, but I don't know if he is gay. He hasn't been around very many girls, and just seems to talk with boys. Though he has given me some signs, like once he kept tapping his foot against mine, and in gym one day, he got an erection in the shower next to me. I'm just not sure. How can I tell? Please help! (I haven't come out yet either.)

Yours truly,
A young gay

Want to correspond?

Many of the essays in this book tell how much the writer wanted to talk or write to someone else. In an effort to meet that need, Alyson Publications will help gay teenagers get in touch with others who would like to correspond. If you'd like to participate in this, please do the following:

1. Get an address where you can receive this mail. If you can use your home address, fine. Otherwise, some possibilities are: (a) ask at the Post Office how much it costs to rent a box there, or whether you can have mail addressed to you at General Delivery in the town where you live, and pick it up at the Post Office; (b) find a friend, perhaps an older gay person, who will let you use their address.

2. Write a letter introducing yourself, and be sure your address is on the letter. Put it in an envelope with a first class postage stamp but without an address. Then put *that* letter and envelope along with a cover letter into a larger envelope and mail it to us:

Alyson Publications (letter exchange)
PO Box 2783
Boston, Mass. 02208

We'll forward this letter to someone else who has expressed interest in exchanging correspondence.

In the cover letter, which will be for our confidential files, you should (a) give your name, address, age and sex; (b) state that you are under 21; (c) give us permission to have mail sent to you; and (d) sign your name at the bottom.

3. When we get your letter, we'll forward it on to someone else who has expressed interest in corresponding. We'll also keep your name on file to later get someone else's letter. Once you've established correspondence with someone you should mail letters directly to them; you'll only go through us to get that initial contact.

4. Be patient. It may take a while to get a first response. If no one replies, it could be that someone has received your letter but is having problems at home or for some other reason isn't able to write back; in that case, try again.

5. There's no charge for this service, but we do ask that it be used only by gays and lesbians under 21 years of age.

Other ALYSON books you'll enjoy

Don't miss our free book offer on the last page

REFLECTIONS OF A ROCK LOBSTER
A story about growing up gay
by Aaron Fricke; $4.95

No one in Cumberland, Rhode Island was surprised when Aaron Fricke showed up at his high school prom with a male date; he had sued his school for the right to do so, and the papers had been full of the news ever since. Yet until his senior year, there would have been nothing to distinguish Aaron Fricke from anyone else his age. You'd never have guessed he was gay — and Aaron did his best to keep it that way. He created a shell around himself as protection against a world that he knew would reject him if it knew the truth. But finally his anger became too great, and he decided to make a stand.

Now, in *Reflections of a Rock Lobster*, you can read Fricke's moving story about growing up gay — about coming to terms with being different, and a lesson in what gay pride can really mean in a small New England town.

TALK BACK!
A gay person's guide to media action
by the Lesbian and Gay Media Advocates; $3.95

When were you last offended by an anti-gay story in the news media? Chances are it hasn't been long; at the time you probably just shrugged your shoulders and thought "there's nothing I can do about it."

Now there *is* something you can do about poor press coverage of our lives. *Talk Back!* tells how you, alone or working with a group, in surprisingly little time can really do something to change the stereotypes that the general public holds of gay men and lesbians.

THE SPARTAN
by Don Harrison; $5.95

Pantarkes' goal is to enter the Olympics and win the laurel crown. But at the age of 16, after accidentally killing the son of a high official, Pantarkes is forced to flee his home in Sparta. For two years his Olympic dreams are postponed as he is drafted into the Theban army to help fight against the invading Macedonians; then finds himself in the middle of a revolt against the Spartan tyrants who had earlier forced him to flee.

This brisk-paced novel provides a vivid picture of classical Greece and the early Olympics, and of an era when gay relationships were a common and valued part of life.

YOUNG, GAY AND PROUD!
edited by Sasha Alyson; $2.95

One high school student in ten is gay. Here is the first book ever to address the problems and needs of that often-invisible minority. It helps young people deal with questions like: Am I really gay? What would my friends think if I told them? Should I tell my parents? Does anybody else feel the way I do?

BETWEEN FRIENDS
by Gillian E. Hanscombe; $5.95

Lillian Faderman, author of *Surpassing the Love of Men*, writes that *"Between Friends* is an achievement. [The author explores] many of the vital lesbian and feminist issues of our day — monogamy, communal living, living with men, sexual relations with men, racism, lesbian motherhood, boy children in the lesbian community, the place of love in a radical movement. She succeeds both in involving the readers in the emotional lives of her characters and demanding of the readers a serious re-examination of their beliefs about the sorts of lives lesbians and feminists ought to be living."

COMING OUT RIGHT
A handbook for the gay male
by William Hanson and Wes Muchmore; $5.95

Any gay man will have no trouble remembering the first time he stepped inside a gay bar. It's a frightening and difficult step, often representing the transition from a life of secrecy and isolation into a world of unknowns.

That step will be easier for gay men who have read *Coming Out Right*. Here, the many facets of gay life are spelled out for the newcomer: how to meet other gay people; what to expect when going home with a gay man; medical problems you could face; employment opportunities and discrimination; getting insurance for gay couples; what to expect at bars, baths and cruising spots; the unique problems faced by men coming out when they're under 18 or over 30. . . . in short, here in one book is information you would otherwise spend years learning the hard way.

THE MEN WITH THE PINK TRIANGLE
by Heinz Heger; $4.95

Here is the true story of a chapter in gay history that has long been hidden from view. In 1939, the author was a young medical student, in love with the son of a Nazi officer. In March of that year the Gestapo abruptly arrested him for homosexuality, and he spent the next six years in concentration camps. Like thousands of other homosexuals, he was forced to wear a pink triangle on his shirt so he could be readily identified for special abuses.

Richard Hall, book columnist for *The Advocate*, praised this as "One of the ten best books of the year" and *Gay Community News* warns that "You may find yourself riveted to your seat" by Heger's narrative.

Most of the books listed here are available in England from Gay Men's Press, PO Box 247, London, N15 6RW.

To get these books:

Ask at your favorite bookstore for the books listed here. You may also order by mail. Just fill out the coupon below, or use your own paper if you prefer not to cut up this book.

GET A FREE BOOK! When you order any two books listed here at the regular price, you may request a **free** copy of *Talk Back!*

BOOKSTORES: Standard trade terms apply. Details and catalog available on request.

Send orders to: **Alyson Publications, Inc.**
PO Box 2783, Dept. B-26
Boston, MA 02208

— — — — — — — — — — — — — — — — — —

Enclosed is $_____ for the following books. (Add $.75 postage when ordering just one book; if you order three or more, we'll pay the postage.)

☐ Between Friends ($5.95)
☐ China House ($4.95)
    A gothic mystery with a gay theme
☐ Coming Out Right ($5.95)
☐ The Men With the Pink Triangle ($4.95)
☐ One Teenager in Ten ($3.95)
☐ Reflections of a Rock Lobster ($4.95)
☐ The Spartan ($5.95)
☐ Talk Back! ($3.95)
☐ Young, Gay and Proud! ($2.95)
☐ Send a free copy of *Talk Back* as offered above. I have ordered at least three other books.

name:_____

address:_____

city:_____ state:_____ zip:_____

ALYSON PUBLICATIONS
PO Box 2783, Dept. B-26, Boston, Mass. 02208